Around the World

IN

80 Years

with

Gordon & Muriel Harrison

Grosvenor House
Publishing Limited

This book is published by
Grosvenor House Publishing Ltd
28-30 High Street, Guildford, Surrey, GU1 3HY.
www.grosvenorhousepublishing.co.uk

A CIP record for this book
is available from the British Library

ISBN 1-905529-88-0

Foreword

Over the years we have realised how little we know about our grandparents, or even much about our parents early life. Unless information is handed down and recorded, it is mostly lost for ever as people pass away. Mindful of this we decided to record the main events and activities of our lives, or at least those we could remember, so that our children and grand-children, and perhaps later generations could see what is after all, history in a personal light, and be made aware of the happiness, and sometimes the sadness, that are a part of every life. It will also hopefully provide an awareness for others, of the need to record for posterity, the details of their lives, and thus provide the basis for our family, on which to build their own histories. That is the philosophy of the following narrative and photos, and we hope everyone who reads it, will find at least some of it, informative and interesting.

Prologue

Gordon's Background

I know very little about either pair of my grandparents and not much about my parent's families, mainly because in my childhood and younger days people were reluctant to talk of family matters to children, and children were not encouraged to ask questions. My paternal grandparents were Samuel Harrison and Jane Wilcock. He had a confectioners business in Barnsley. I never met him as he died before Mum and Dad married, and she visited us only once when I was a schoolboy living in Portsmouth. I have no knowledge of their dates and places of birth, death, or marriage They lived all their lives in Yorkshire..

My father Reginald Gordon Harrison was born on 23rd March 1885 in Barnsley. He was not a tall man and this was attributed to the fact that he contracted polio as a child, something I was unaware of until Pat told me while I was writing these notes. I cannot remember him having any real hobbies or interest, and he never to my knowledge took part in any sport other than a social game of tennis. This also was probably a legacy of his childhood illness. He disliked gardening and left any house decorating to mum, but he was an excellent cook and I remember he always made the Christmas cakes and puddings.

Dad was a member of quite a large family. An old family photograph circa 1910 (Fig.1) which I hold shows Dad at the back right side with his mother and 4 brothers (William, Charles, Stanley, and Douglas) and 3 sisters (Edith, Florence and Jane), and this information only came my way with the photo I inherited, on the occasion of mum's death a few years ago. The photo does not include my Grandfather, who had died earlier. Apart from his sister Edie whom I met just once, I also met my Grandmother only once when they visited us at Portsmouth in the 1930's. I understand it was my Grandmother who had money and owned the bakery/confectionery shops in Barnsley and Doncaster.

Pat my sister, believes there was another brother, the black sheep of the family, who was dispatched to America, and who made a lot of money there in connection with Fox Films. When he died intestate, Grandma in true Victorian fashion, refused to have anything to do with his large estate, and didn't tell any of the family about it until it was too late to make a claim.

My maternal Grandparents were William Henry Bellingham and Laura Ellen Crutchfield, who was apparently one of twins. She died in June 1934 aged 70, and my grandfather died in November 1951 aged 86. Although they lived in Brighton a short distance from Portsmouth, I never met them. I know from records and photographs that he was a Captain in the RAMC. and there is a picture of him at (Fig2)

My mother Kathleen Bellingham was born on 19th.November 1890 at a place called Barham East Hothy, Framfield in Sussex. She was of medium height and was the most kind and caring person I ever knew. I know even less of her background and early years than I do of Dad's. Mum had two sisters, one named Ada who lived in London, and another named Ruby who lived with her father in Brighton, and also two brothers Laurie, and Bill. Bill nicknamed "Ching", and Laurie nicknamed "Flop", were both pilots in the RFC during the first world war. After the war both were required to drop rank if they wanted to stay in the service, which Laurie did. Bill didn't want to and emigrated to Canada . (Bill's sons both joined the RAF at the outbreak of the second world war, and one of them was shot down over Belgium) During this war, Bill sent Mum some Red Cross parcels, to help out with the rations. I seem to remember meeting both of Mum's sisters on one occasion, but never the brothers

I believe Mum and Dad met in South Africa, when he was in the army, and she was an army officer's daughter. They married at the Register Office in Winchester on 26th April 1910, when he was 25 and she was 19. Dad was in the RAMC, and working in the military hospital there. Dad spent 4 years during the first world war in the BEF in France, where he was gassed, and from which he later suffered from coughing fits, when he could not get his breath. Most of the rest of Dad's army service was at home, although Mum and Dad did spend a year in Bermuda, just after the first war, where Mum did some teaching I have a photograph of Mum and Dad together dated 5th August 1915 (Fig 3), and have Dad's 3 Great war medals, and his long service and good conduct medal. Dad retired from the army on 29th. December 1925, when he was working at the Queen Alexandra hospital in Portsmouth, and we went to live at 24 Hartley Rd. North End Portsmouth. I was 3 years old at the time, and I have no real memories before this date.

After Dad retired he got a job as a dispenser, at the practice of Doctor Thomas at London Road Portsmouth, and he worked there until Doctor Thomas retired about 1936/7. After a period of unemployment with the war approaching, he got a job at the Airspeed works at Portsmouth Airport. I am not sure what exactly he did there, but he worked there during the 1939-1945 war.

Living and working in the waterlogged trenches in the first world war had a far reaching effect on him, and was the direct cause of the neuritis he suffered later in life, when his hands and legs stopped working properly. He was unable to hold things and to walk without help, and moved around the house in a wheel chair. For many years Mum had to manhandle him everywhere, until he died in 1960, of disseminated sclerosis, at the Queen Alexandra hospital, where he had held his last appointment, before he retired from the army. The hospital had by now transferred to the NHS.

After years of moving Dad around, Mum was now relieved of this task, and had many years of peace, until she joined Dad, when she died of heart failure, also at the Queen Alexandra hospital in 1986, aged 95. Fortunately my sister Pat and Mum lived in adjacent old people's bungalows during Mum's latter years, and Pat was able to help Mum. Both Mum and Dad were cremated at the Portchester Crematorium, and have a joint entry in the Book of Remembrance there.

Muriel's Background

I know very little about my paternal grandparents, only that they were married in 1891, and celebrated their golden wedding anniversary in 1941. (Fig 5) I called them Gran. and Gramps, and remember them as being very pleasant, and fairly quiet people. They had 3 children, 2 daughters and a son, my father They lived in a small terrace house in Cardigan Rd. Portsmouth, and I remember all the family playing games, like passing a ring around in the front room of the house, and having to guess who had it when the music stopped. In those days people only used their front room for visitors and family gatherings, and it wasn't used at other times. I remember their bedroom had several stuffed animals, and birds in domed glass cases, popular in Victorian times, and I hated them. I still do not like stuffed animals as ornaments, I would rather see them alive.(so Damien Hurst has done nothing new) .

I know a little more about my maternal Grandparents (Fig 6) since I lived with them for 7 or 8 years, and I gathered a little information about them from my mother. I called them Nana and Pops. Mum thought that Nana had originally come from the Cheshire area. Her maiden name was Mary Jane Blades, and her birthday was 12th. August. Pop's name was Walter Isaac Higgins, and was born in Hambledon in Hampshire on 25th. January 1874, of Irish parents. He left school at the age of 10 years to work on a farm. My mother remembered visiting pop's parents on one occasion, and had one memory of them visiting Nana and Pops in Foster Rd. Portsmouth. Mum said that Pop's mother was a little old lady in a long black dress, and a lace apron, with a little lace cap on her head. His father was fairly tall, and had black hair and a black beard, and was dressed in a black suit, with a frock coat and a black top hat, and being a child she was terrified of him. Pops must have had a brother or brothers, as they tormented their mother when she was losing her sight, by hiding the freshly laundered washing, so she couldn't find it. When I was a child I would ask Pops about his boyhood, and each time he started to tell me, Nana would come in and tell him to stop, saying "she doesn't want to know all that rubbish", and Pops would stop and not tell me any more, but I did want to know very much. Pops did not write all that well, probably due to his brief education at a village school in Hambledon. This was the village where cricket was first played, and it boasted a pub called either "The Cricketers" or "The Bat and Ball"

Nana and Pops lived at 36 Foster Rd, Portsmouth, and had two daughters, Birdie and Elsie Gladys my Mother, (Fig 4) who was 18 months younger than Birdie. Nana used to sing around the house while she was working, and Pop's nickname for her was "Birdie". I never heard him call her Mary. I suppose that's how Auntie Birdie got her name.

CHAPTER 1

Gordon - The early years

I was born in the Princess Margaret hospital in Aldershot, on 1st.January 1923. My earliest memories are however living at No.24 Hartley Road, North End, Portsmouth when I was about 3 years old. This was a semi- detached Council house with 3 rooms downstairs, 3 bedrooms and a bathroom, which not every house had in those days. My bedroom was the small front bedroom. I was the youngest of 4 children, having one brother Reg, and 2 sisters, Pat and Dorothy. Reg had joined the army when he was 14, so I did not see much of him, except when he came home on leave. He shared my bedroom then, and I shared his cigarette smoke, but we didn't think of things like that in those days. Pat and Dorothy were both at Stamshaw school with me, but I didn't see much of them, Pat being about 14 when I joined, and Dorothy was 2 years older than me. We had a fairly small garden, but I remember we kept chickens and had raspberry, loganberry, black and red currant and gooseberry bushes. Unlike most houses at that time, the room we kept for visitors etc was at the back, and we lived in the front room. I remember this living room had a range, with a small oven for our fire,.and mum did some cooking on this. Unfortunately it had to be black leaded when it wasn't in use. In the kitchen we had a gas cooker, and a copper which was used for washing. I can't remember how it was heated, but as we had a gas supply, I assume the water in the copper was heated in this way. The copper had other uses. It was also used for boiling the suet puddings in an earthenware basin with a white cloth tied to the top. Presumably this was why our suet puddings were always soggy.

Mum and Dad would not visit the local pub "The Green Posts", but were happy to make their own stout in the copper. The hops and oats mixture, which came in a large yellow packet, was put in the copper, boiling water was put in, and yeast put in on top to ferment it. After a few days you skimmed off the yeast, and bottled the remaining liquid, which my mother would not call stout, but Brew. (so there is nothing new about home brewing) I remember they did lose a few bottles, which had a tendency to explode. I can also remember two Dutch looking paintings, which we had for many years, and a very large rosewood circular dining table in the back room. There was no central heating in those days, and all our rooms had open fires, the ashes for which had to be cleaned out every morning, before lighting the next fire. The coal for the fires was delivered by sack by the coalman, and fortunately, unlike some houses where the coalman had to tramp through the house, we had access to our coal cellar which was part of our kitchen, through a side way. Because all the rooms were cold in winter, apart from the living room, I can remember my mother heating a garden brick in the oven, and wrapping it in paper, before putting it in my bed. This was the era before hot water bottles came into use, but the brick certainly seemed to do the trick.

An aspect of home delivery which I remember was the sale of onions. The French "onion johnies" as they were called, suitably attired in striped jerseys and berets, would push their bicycles round the streets, with strings of onions attached to their handlebars and crossbar, and try to sell them door to door. How they made a profit is a mystery, as their onions were shipped in bulk, and stored at various sites along the south coast, before being hawked round the streets. They must have been successful however, because they arrived every year (excluding the war years) and I understand carried on during the late 1940's and early 1950's.

When I was 5 years old I was taken to Stamshaw School by an older girl, who also lived in my road. My first teacher was a Miss Wearn, who had a habit of leaning over the double desks, and displaying her 'directoire' knickers. I thought she was old and crotchety, and much preferred our other teacher (Miss Jones), who was younger and attractive. (even at 5 years old you notice these things). During my first week at school a friend Kenny Abbott heard my name being read out, and went home and told his parents that there was a boy in his class called Golden! I was invited to his house, and I think his parents were a little disappointed to discover my real name. Ken and I played football and cricket together at junior school. His parents owned a fruit and vegetable shop, and Ken would help his parents to deliver orders on Saturdays. I occasionally helped out, although Mum wasn't keen on me acting as errand boy. Ken was killed in the war along with a number of my other school friends, but I never knew how or where.

In these days most food deliveries were carried out by errand boys on bikes or by tradesmen with horse and cart. Our bread (unwrapped) came in this way, and our milkman had a small 2 wheel horse drawn cart, with a large churn on it, from which he dispensed the milk directly to the customer's milk jug, with a large metal ladle. The postman made two deliveries a day, collections were made at certain boxes until 10 o'clock at night, and even from these, next morning delivery was guaranteed. Saturday collection and delivery was normal, and even on Sunday the 4 pm collection ensured next day delivery. Mum often wrote her letters on Sunday afternoon, and I or Dorothy posted them.

Most boys in the 5-7 age group had comics delivered to the door, with the newspapers. I had the Tiger Comic, but the oldest and most famous was "Comic Cuts". For the 7-11 age group there were daily boy's magazines like the Adventure, Skipper, Wizard, Rover and Hotspur. I got the Wizard every Wednesday, and when I had finished reading it from cover to cover, swapped it for the Hotspur. The Wizard was mostly adventure stories, but the Hotspur was mostly school stories. These school stories were very popular, because most boys had never been to, or were likely to go to, a boarding school, and the friendships, rivalries and dorm. feasts made for avid reading. Even today the stories of Harry Potter are similar, and I have always thought, that J.K.Rowling must have based her stories on these, but with a bit of magic thrown in. You have to remember that at this time there were few radios, and no television. Because of this boys had to make their own entertainment. Sport was predominant, but we were inveterate collectors of conkers in the autumn, which we played at home, and in the playground. We also collected cigarette cards. All the major cigarette companies at this time produced these, in series of 50, including sportsmen, Kings and Queens, film stars etc., and we bartered them to get the full collection, which could be put into albums provided by the cigarette manufacturers. We also played 'fag cards' with them. This was a game where one card was set up vertically against a wall, and you took turns to flick your cards at the set up card, and the one who knocked it down, collected all the other cards on the ground. We also collected and swapped foreign stamps, and my original album (which cost 6d and which I still have) was the basis of my collection, which I carried on over the years. What happens to it in future is anybody's guess.

When I was about 6 years old, there was an epidemic of measles, which I contracted, which left me with an eye that turned, and required me to wear glasses. I continued to wear these until I was about 15, when I left them off, but I had to return to wearing them later in life. I had two friends who lived at no.16 Hartley Rd., Jack and Arthur Webb, and Jack and I continued our friendship for many years. Mum liked to get us out as much as time and money would allow, and once a year she would take Jack, Arthur and I to a picnic, on the old ramparts at Hilsea. We always had the usual egg, tomato and cucumber sandwiches, but we enjoyed eating outside, until we became too busy doing our own thing.

A common article of dress for boys in those days, was a belt of material about 2inches wide, with 3 stripes, red and black, red and white or green and white. These belts were fixed by an S shaped metal snake, which fitted in a round clip, and these were used until you graduated into long trousers about the age of 10 or 11, when you used braces On Sundays Dorothy and I were dressed up in our best clothes (the only time we were allowed to wear them), and sent to Sunday school, until we were old enough to complain that we were too old for that sort of thing.

On summer evenings Mum, Dad, Dorothy and I would often go for walks or trips on the tram. One of our favourite trips, was to the hard at the dockyard gate, to see the mudlarks searching in the mud for pennies that had been thrown to them. To get there we had to pass through some poor areas, and because we were togged up in our Sunday best, we got some raucous and rude remarks thrown at us—how embarrassing!. At Easter we were taken for our annual hike over Portsdown hill, and the usual picnic sandwiches were produced. Dad always complained that he was too tired by the time we had climbed the hill, and said he would wait there for us. I wondered if the proximity of the George Inn, situated nearby, caused his fatigue. As I got older I was out all day long in summer, only coming home in the evening for meals. In those days children were safe almost anywhere, and parents did not worry where we were, or what we were doing, although if they had known, they would not have been so complacent. (To reach our camping and bonfire site we had to cross an electrified railway line)

A very sad sight frequently seen between the wars, was of ex-service men wearing their medals, begging on the pavements, and going round the streets singing for money. After the first world war these men were initially called heroes, and told they would come back to a land, fit for heroes to live in. The reality was different, and because the jobs they had left were not guaranteed after the war, many remained unemployed. Also many had lost limbs in the service of their country, and for a time some of these had to resort to begging, and the generosity of passers by. Eventually the British Limbless ex-Service Men's Association (BLESMA) was formed to help these men, but high unemployment, and strikes in the late 1920's and the early 1930's, did not help matters. Rudyard Kipling wrote a poem called 'Tommy' about this situation, and how the public appreciation of soldiers in peacetime, differed so markedly from that in wartime. Fortunately this situation was not repeated after 1945.

When I was 7 I transferred to the junior school, with an old, but very motherly teacher Miss Good. I was a fairly good reader at this age, and I remember helping two other boys –Capel and Howes- with individual reading. It was at this time that I first took an interest in sport, running in the combined Portsmouth schools, 60 yards junior sports day, at Alexandra Park, but without success. Jack and I would go regularly, to watch the school football team play, at the local Gas Co. Ground, and in summer, the cricket team at Alexandra Park.

My sister Pat left school at 14 and got a job at a haberdashers named Johnstone George, not far from our house in Hartley Rd.

The price of practically everything in the shop ended in 11 pence three farthings, usually called eleven three, and the farthing change if not available in the till, would be a packet of pins. You can still see this pricing philosophy today, when items are invariably marked £- 99p. Pat worked long hours, up to 9 o'clock and 10 o'clock on Fridays and Saturdays, but she did get Sunday and Wednesday afternoon off, when she went to the cinema, or the pictures as we called it then. We couldn't afford holidays in those days, but as we attended Sunday school at the Hilsea Garrison church, we went on their annual outings, usually in an open char-a-banc, but also on the trams, which operated between Portsmouth and Horndean (called the Horndean Light Railway) These were also open on top. My friends Jack and Arthur Webb, did actually go on holiday once to Stubbington, a village near Portsmouth, with an uncle who came down in an old Austin 7 saloon to pick them up. This caused quite a stir in the street, and they were seen off by a crowd of cheering boys and girls who lived nearby.

My next teacher in the junior school was a Mr.Cronin. His classroom led off the Hall, where there was a stage, on which the school orchestra practised each morning, for summer and Christmas concerts. I remember being note perfect with Schubert's Rosamunde Overture, and it is probably from this time, that I began to acquire my love of classical music. My form teacher was a gifted painter, who painted the large posters advertising the school Christmas concerts during our lessons. Not only was it interesting to see the pirate with a hook and eye patch developing, it also made for easy lessons while he was painting. For this Christmas concert, we also spent many hours listening to the senior boys practising the songs about a pirate ship, with its black flag appearing on the starboard bow. My last few months at Stamshaw school were with another form master

Mr. Threadingham.. His class is only remembered for swimming lessons, which I wasn't good at, but it took us out of the classroom, mental arithmetic, which we all hated, and spelling tests which I was good at.

Stamshaw school which I was soon to leave, was an old turn of the century school, with smoky open fires, and the forms banked up, with the back row higher than the front. While the back rows were much further from the eagle eye of the form master, and the occasional missile in the form of a piece of chalk or blackboard duster, they were also colder, because there was only a coal fire at the front of the classroom, where the schoolmaster was positioned!! Your position was decided by regular tests, so you had no choice in the matter. We had a large playground, in which we played football during PE lessons, which was very popular. There was also a large metal shed for shelter when it was raining, but as the lavatories were also outside, we got wet going there instead. All the masters in the junior school had canes, and were not afraid to use them. I had a few sore hands in my time, but unlike today we didn't tell our parents about it, because we knew they would not be sympathetic, and merely say "you must have deserved it"

Most children were expected to learn a musical instrument, and both Pat and Dorothy played!! Dad's violin. Perhaps because I had a lot of homework to do, I managed to escape this burden.

Christmas was a pleasant time for us. Shops only decorated during December, and I can't remember any street decorations. We made our own paper chains to decorate the room, and did our personal shopping, only a few days before Christmas, leaving some of the perishables to be bought on Christmas Eve. Because we only had a little pocket money, our presents, usually obtained from Woolworths, were similarly small. I was an avid reader even in those days, and each Christmas for a number of years I was given the same two "Annuals". Christmas morning was spent reading, and consuming most of the sweets, which appeared in our stockings. Dad always made the Christmas puddings and cakes. I enjoyed the Christmas dinner, which was usually chicken, a treat in those days, and I always managed to find the threepenny bit, in the pudding, but by teatime, I had stuffed myself so much, I usually felt too bloated and slightly sick, to enjoy the tinned fruit and cake. Dad always baked a cake for my birthday, when he cooked the Christmas cake, so I never went without. I also never went without birthday presents on my birthday, New Years Day, even though it was very close to Christmas. I can remember Mum had very positive ideas about decorations, and they always had to come down on New Years Eve, to start the new year right, she said.

CHAPTER 2

Muriel – The early years

I was born at 29 Foster Rd.Landport Portsmouth, in a terrace house, in a road of mainly terrace houses. The house consisted of 3 downstairs living rooms, and a scullery(the forerunner of the modern utility room), 3 bedrooms but no bathroom. I was baptised at St Mary's Church Fratton, where my parents were married. It was a large church situated opposite Church Road, where my mother lived in later years, during war time.

I am not sure when my parents were married, but I think my Mother was about 22 years old. As my mother was born on 6th. June 1900 this would have been 1922. My mother was not very tall, had blue eyes and light brown hair. She was a pretty woman with a fair skin. My mother had one sister, 18 months older than her called Birdie. As was the fashion in those days, girls in their teens were taught music, and Birdie learned to play the piano, and mandolin, and my mother had singing lessons, and learned to play the violin. Mum had a strong mezzo soprano voice, and I heard her sing on one or two occasions when I was little, rattling some empty glasses on a table, with the vibration of her voice.

There was a lovely photo on the piano of my mother, taken when she was 18, It disappeared, and unfortunately, neither my sister Greta, nor I, found it when my mother passed away. In the photo she was wearing a pendant, which I now have, which was sent to her from Canada by her fiancee. My mother had many admirers as a young woman, and became engaged when she was 17, to Billy, a pilot in the RCAF, when he was stationed in England, during the first world war. Its surprising that Nana and Pops consented to her engagement, because when Billy had to return to Canada, he sent for my mother, but they refused to let her go, so that was the end of that romance. Mum had a beautiful diamond engagement ring,Billy had given her, but I don't remember her ever wearing it. (more about that later)

My mother's admirers took her out often to the theatre, and always took her in a taxi, and bought chocolates for the evening, all done properly, so that Nana and Pops were kept happy. Mum was also brought home again by taxi, at a reasonable time. They always got Pop's permission before taking his daughter out. Often boxes of chocolates would be sent to the house, and Mum would come home from work to find the box opened, and Nana and Auntie Birdie eating the chocolates.

My mother worked as a seamstress from 8 am to 8 pm in a Gents outfitters. Auntie Birdie also worked for a Gents outfitters. Nana and Auntie Birdie were the dominant members of the family, and Nana seemed to favour Birdie, rather than my mother. Maybe Pops favoured my mother, but I doubt it from what I experienced myself. Pops had chickens in the garden, and Mum remembered on one occasion, Pops asking her if she had enjoyed her boiled egg that morning. Mum being young said "what egg", so the cat was out of the bag, and Nana and Pops had a row, when he found out that Nana gave most of the eggs away to neighbours, and people coming to the door begging. Nana was very fond of giving things away to beggars, and Pops was not pleased.

My father's name was James Henry Hayden. He had dark brown wavy hair, and was of average height. I have no knowledge of my father's birth date, not even the year He was in the army during the first world war, in the Cycling Corps of the Hampshire Regiment, and served in Russia where he saw the Cossacks, and said they were really cruel to the Russian people, and of fierce appearance. After the war he worked as a sorting clerk in the GPO at Portsmouth, after passing a Civil Service exam to get the post, and coming top of the exam list. My father had two sisters Nell and Annie, who both married men who had served in the army in the first world war. Auntie Nell married Fred Tuck, and they lived in North End in a fairly big house with a forecourt. The front downstairs rooms were divided in two by folding doors, which were opened to make a large room for parties etc. The room at the back had a lot of cartoon drawings on the wall, of my uncles, and other army men, all drawn by my father. The room at the back had a kitchen, with beyond it a conservatory full of geraniums, and a medium sized garden. I have a strong memory of the smell of these geraniums which pervaded the rooms downstairs. Auntie Nell and Uncle Fred had no children, but I remember Uncle Fred's waxed military moustache, pointed at the ends like Hercule Poirot. My father's other sister Auntie Annie was married to Bert Townley, and they lived in a fair sized house in New Road Copnor. Uncle Bert also had a moustache, but not as military as Uncle Fred's. They had twin daughters Brenda and Joan, who were not a bit alike. My cousin Brenda played the piano very well, and taught me to play for a year, from the age of 9 on Nana and Pop's piano, when I was living in 36 Foster Road .I remember pounding away practising my scales

In those days families did not talk about their background or past experiences, particularly to a child, so I did not learn much from them. When I was a schoolgirl, each time I asked, I was told "children should be seen and not heard" I cannot remember much about my parent's house in Foster Road, having left it at the age of 7 or thereabouts. In the front room on the mantle piece was a gold coloured clock, with a revolving pendulum in a glass domed case. Above that was a painting by my father, of our grey tabby Persian cat called Bimbo. One of my earliest memories is of being bathed by my mother, in the large galvanised bath in the kitchen (with no bathroom we all used this for bathing), and as quick as can be, as my mother lifted me out of the bath I picked up Bimbo and put him in the bath water. My mother was not pleased.

Another memory is of falling down the stairs. The staircase had a bend at the top, and I was just negotiating this, when I heard my mother speak. I looked round and was so taken by her hat, that I didn't look where I was going. The hat was so pretty consisting entirely of mauve velvet violets made into a fitted cap. I was only a toddler and fell. I also remember my father being fond of the radio. He made his own, and spent a lot of time fiddling with radio sets. He also had a banjo which he played at parties. Sometimes on the radio they played Three Blind Mice, and when it got to the part where they had their tails cut off, I always cried, which made my father laugh.

The middle room downstairs at 29 Foster Rd. had a glass fronted cupboard, in which there was a glass decanter of red wine, and the colour always attracted me. I can remember my parents going to dances and smart evenings out, my father in a dress suit and my mother wearing lovely evening dresses, mid calf or almost full length as was fashionable in the 1920's. One of her dresses was made from red lace over taffeta, worn with a red velvet longish jacket, with a white fur collar, red satin court shoes, and matching handbag. Another dress was of yellow flowered taffeta and yellow georgette, which was cut down for me by Auntie Birdie when I was about 9 years old.

I slept in the middle bedroom with my own suite of child sized furniture. I had a tortoiseshell backed dressing table set. My mother had such pretty china, white with little pink rosebuds and gold rims. At Christmas Mum always bought very elaborate crackers and large boxes of chocolates, and one year I had a silver and white fairy doll. My mother would go out to nice restaurants, where the waitresses wore black dresses with lacy aprons, and little lace caps on their heads, and take me with her. We would order lovely cream cakes and chocolate éclairs. I decided I wanted to be a waitress when I grew up. Mum said that I would change my mind, but I did have a waitress outfit one Christmas.

There was an epidemic of measles when I was 5 years old, and I was very ill with it. Mum said my eyes were stuck together, and I couldn't see for 2 weeks. I remember having nightmares, and hated the castor oil the doctor made me take. After measles I had to wear glasses and have done ever since. I believe the Beadle came to the house to ask why I was not at school during my recuperation.

I started school when I was just over 5 years old, and I attended a small private school called Magdala Academy (I suspect it was my father's choice), which was within walking distance, as we did not have a car, very few people did in those days. It was a mixed school, and I had lots of friends there, but my closest was Barbara Kilbury who was the same age as me, and we started school together. She was an only child, and lived nearby in my road. All her family were good swimmers, and used to go to Eastney, a local beach to swim. Her parents had a car (the only people I knew who had one), and they took their beach tent and deck chairs on to the beach on Sundays in summer, and often took me with them, as none of my family could swim. Barbara and I would lie on the beach watching the ocean liners and big ships in the channel, and waiting for the big waves to wash over us, as the wash from the ships reached the shore. Barbara could swim could but I couldn't, and I used a rubber ring to keep afloat. One day when a big wave knocked me over I panicked, and Barbara's father grabbed me and said this wont do, and started to teach me to swim by showing me how the salt water would keep you afloat. I have always felt very grateful to him for teaching me, and giving me confidence in the water. I can't remember but I suppose my mother took me to school and back. There were no school dinners then, so we went home for dinner. School was 9 am till noon, $1^1/_2$ hours for lunch, then lessons again from 1.30pm till 4pm. We had Wednesday afternoons off for art homework, and school from 9am till noon on Saturday Nana and Pops lived at 36 Foster Rd. opposite my parent's house (a bad mistake on my parents part), where my mother and Auntie Birdie were brought up. I'm not sure where Auntie Birdie lived when I was little.

The headmaster of Magdala academy was Mr.Davies. He was very strict and had a cane for punishment, which he used on the hands of the boys, but only on the shoulders of the girls. I winced every time a boy's hand was struck, as I was in the front row. Heating was provided by one coal fire, and as the teacher stood in front of the fire by the blackboard, it was often very cold. I remember my mother keeping a cane in the house, but don't remember her ever using it. It was probably only a threat. The school had a yard at the back to play in, during the short playtime in the morning and afternoon. Two lavatories were in the yard ,not the building as it was a small Victorian building. I recall there was one teacher Miss Baker, I didn't like very much. You couldn't control small children today in such surroundings, but discipline was strict in those days. You received punishment by writing lines, which were written on the blackboard for offenders to copy. School uniform in the winter included a navy velour hat, gymslip, white blouse, and black shoes and stockings, while in the summer we wore white Panama hats, ordinary dresses, blazers, and short white socks. The blazers and hats bore the school badge. After the age of 11 we played netball at Alexandra park. We had quite a lot of homework, and my best subjects were art, history, geography, and spelling. I found maths very difficult, and algebra was a no-no. After the age of 11 or 12 the school taught typing, shorthand, book keeping, and tracing, which was basic training for children, whose parents wanted them to enter the Civil Service.

Suddenly things changed, but I didn't realise at that age what had happened, being too young to be told! When I was about 7 years old my mother left my father (and her home and me), and I went to live with Nana and Pops. They were very kind to me, and of course Auntie Birdie was there a lot. I really loved my Pops, and would sit on his lap playing with his gold watch and chain on his waistcoat. The chain had a gold $1^1/_2$ sovereign, and a mother of pearl pendant on it. (Neil now has the coin) Pops would talk to me about the animals on the farm, and animals he had owned, and I am sure that I inherited my love of animals from him. I loved Pops very much, and often told him that when I grew up I was going to marry him!! At that time Nana and Pops kept chickens at the bottom of the garden, a black and white Pomeranian dog called Jackie, a yellow tabby cat called Teewee, and 5 caged birds.—2 goldfinches and 3 canaries which were in their cages hanging up in the kitchen window. Nana's house had a deep white step and a brass one leading into the house, and Nana was very proud of them, forever whitening the step and polishing the brass, so I had to step over them when I entered the house. Whenever I came home, I was met by Teewee the cat waiting for me.

The front room was kept for visitors, and only used at Christmas, and had sash windows with thick lace curtains, and wooden venetian blinds. The fireplace had a big brass fender and a brass companion set, and it was Pop's job to clean it all on Sunday. On the wide mantelpiece was a picture of me as a toddler on the beach. The piano had a photo of my mother and a small silver cup, which Pops had won with his racing pigeons. It had Seaview and the year engraved on it. The piano had brass candle holders, and there were many pictures on the walls. There was a glass fronted dresser, with a photo of my parents on their wedding day on it. Mum's clothes were typical of the day, like those worn by the queen Mum on her wedding day, when she was Duchess of York The room we lived in, the kitchen, always had a fire alight in the winter. There was a Philips radio, and Pop's songbirds in a cage were hanging in the window. The mantelpiece had a black cloth, painted with leaves and roses by my father.

The scullery had a deep butler sink, copper boiler, and gas cooker, and a dresser full of china and glass. Outside the back door was a lavatory and wash house, which had a mangle, and galvanised bowls and a bath.

The garden had my swing, flower borders, a chicken house, and fruit bushes. It was sometimes my job to collect the eggs, and pick the raspberries and loganberries. The gardens were separated by 5ft. brick walls. Pops loved flowers, and had marguerites, snapdragons, hollyhocks, asters, golden rod and roses, and there were always butterflies and ladybirds there. My bedroom at the front of the house had a big iron bedstead with brass knobs, and a marble top washstand, with a china bowl and jug, a wicker chair, and lace curtains. The bed had a feather mattress with flannelette sheets, and an eiderdown. When I left my parents home, I took with me a child's chair, which is now in the back bedroom of our present house, my lovely cuddly toy dog, and a soft "dolly dimple" in a white and mauve skating outfit. I always took the doll to bed with me, and the dog sat on the wicker chair next to the bed. The child's chair was kept in the kitchen.

Keeping a house clean in those days was very hard work, as there were no vacuum cleaners or electric gadgets, just a carpet sweeper, broom, dustpan and brush, and dusters. Nana had a flat-iron to iron the washing, which was heated on the open fire or the gas stove, and required a thick cloth holder. To check if the iron was hot enough, women would spit on the iron, and if the spit disappeared in a bubble of steam it was hot enough. Carpets and rugs were hung over the washing line, and beaten with a beater made from rattan or bamboo. Fire grates had to be cleaned out every morning, and the grate black leaded. Washing day was quite a performance. The passage had linoleum on the floor, and Nana would put newspaper down, so it wouldn't get dirty or wet, and the same thing happened when the coalman delivered the coal. When I got home from school on Mondays, Nana would get me to help her to pull the sheets after drying, so she could fold them. The washing was washed in the copper, in which suet pudding was also cooked in a basin covered with a white cloth. After drying in winter, the washing was aired on a wooden clothes horse in front of the kitchen fire. Lunch on Monday was always left over meat from the Sunday roast, lumpy mashed potatoes and processed peas. Nana was not a good cook, neither was Auntie Birdie, but Mum was a very good cook (ask Gordon about her apple pies)

Our milk was delivered every morning in a churn from which it was ladled into our china jug. Our greengrocer came round with a horse drawn cart, and on one occasion when I saw Mr. Kirby the greengrocer hitting the horse, I shouted at him. I bet he thought I was a cheeky child, and I probably was. The baker's boy delivered bread from a basket on his bicycle, and errand boys on bicycles were commonplace. There was a grocery shop near our house, and I would pop in there to buy ice cream in a jug, and into the local cake shop to buy a penny bun, or a Chelsea bun.

Most men smoked in those days, and Pops rolled his own cigarettes in a little rolling machine. I would sometimes run an errand to buy his Rizla cigarette papers, and his Digger Shag, and Gold Block tobacco. Occasionally I was sent to the local pub which had a "bottle and jug" entrance, to buy Pops a jug of mild and bitter ale. There were not many cars about then, and we used trams, or double decker buses, or we walked. Nana and Pops had electricity in their house, but there were still gas mantels in the kitchen. I can remember Pops lighting them, and replacing them.

During my first two or three years with Nana and Pops, I did not see much of my mother. At her divorce Mum got all the blame, and even her own family turned against her, so she didn't come to Nana and Pops house until I was about 11 years old Occasionally she would meet me from school, and then go back to her house. My father would come to the house sometimes at dinner time, and Nana would give him a meal. I once heard Nana and Birdie who was at the house quite often, talking about my mother, and said, 'stop talking about my mother like that'. Thereafter they were more careful. When I was about 9, my father said he would take me to a lady he wanted me to meet. All innocent I thought nothing of it, and assumed her to be just a friend. She was named Adelaide (Addie), and she worked as a barmaid at a pub called Martha Brickwoods. I went to see her a few times, and to Putney to see her family. One Christmas she bought me a pink taffeta party dress. This did not go down well with Auntie Birdie, who had already made me a blue taffeta one, and the pink one disappeared.(I didn't like it much anyway). Auntie Birdie made me a new party dress every Christmas, and it was the first thing I saw when I woke. She was very good to me, and after the age of 12, she made me long party dresses. While I was living with my grandparents, they took me with them to social evenings, where I learned to dance. Old Tyme dancing as it was called, was very popular in the 1920's and 1930's, with lots of dance bands playing in local halls, hotels and on the wireless. I enjoyed dancing, and I was to have plenty of opportunities to attend dances, with my friend Barbara.

When I was about 10 my father said he was getting married to Addie, and bought a house in Meredith Rd. Hilsea. He asked me if I liked the wallpaper in my bedroom, and I thought he meant me to visit and sleep there sometimes. The paper was childish, and more appropriate for a boy, as it had trains on it. One day he announced there was to be a party at the new house, and I and my best friend Barbara were invited. It turned out to be the day of the wedding to Addie, but not having been to the wedding, I didn't know what it was all about. A few days later my father came to take me to live with him. He brought his sister Nell, and Auntie Birdie was there with Barbara's mother. There was a big scene. I didn't want to go, and I said I wasn't going to live with them. I spent the time crying in sheer misery, as I wanted to stay with Nana and Pops. My father tried to bribe me by saying I could go to the same school, and Barbara and my friends could come and visit me. I think I had realised that I wouldn't be able to stay at the same school, which was too far to walk to and from the new house, four times a day. Barbara's mother said she wouldn't have anything to do with persuading me. I don't remember Auntie Birdie, Auntie Nell, or Nana saying very much, but Pops wouldn't force me to go, and said I could stay with them if I wanted to .My father's lack of understanding of a 10 year old child's feelings still appals me. It was a big decision for Nana and Pops to take, since they were elderly, and I was a big responsibility, and expense. I don't know if my father gave them any money for my keep, but he should have done.

It was only when I was older, that I realised what a drain I must have been on my grandparents finances. I think my father paid for my education, until I refused to live with him and Addie, and Auntie Birdie must have helped by making my clothes. Pops was a boilermaker in the dockyard, and when he retired, he worked in Brickwood's brewery, hard work for an elderly man. Nana took in lodgers, always Navy families, when the husband's ship was in the dockyard. for repair. One family that came often were Bob and Flo Bartlett, with a son about the same age as me named Leslie. Mrs Bartlett was very nice, and would take me and Leslie to the dockyard gate to meet her husband, when he came off his ship. I kept in touch with Mrs. Bartlett for some years. Eventually Leslie followed his father into the navy, and when we were in Singapore in the 1950's, and Neil was a little boy, Leslie and his wife Stella and their daughter Linda were posted to Singapore, so we were able to renew our acquaintance. They now live in Gloucester, and I still keep in touch with them every Christmas.

Apart from my ordeal when my father wanted me to live with him, I had other unpleasant experiences. I must have been very cheeky, and said something to Nana, and went out of the door slamming it behind me. Nana called me back, and gave me a hard slap on the face. When Auntie Birdie came in the evening, she marched me upstairs, threw me on the bed, and gave me a thorough good hiding. I cried myself to sleep that night. On another occasion, probably on my birthday, I woke to find my lovely cuddly dog had gone, and in its place was a fully dressed baby doll. I don't ever recall playing with it, as I was not a dolly type of child. Later I tried to find out where my dog had gone, but I think Nana had given it away to a child in the street. I never forgave her for that.

Pops tried to help me with my maths homework (the blind leading the blind), because I found it so difficult. We had mental arithmetic at school which helped with my maths, but there was always the fear of looking a fool if you gave the wrong answer. We were also set problems from old Civil Service exam papers, but I much preferred history, geography and art. Nana had a rest on Wednesday afternoons when I did my homework, and I had to keep very quiet or there would be trouble.

CHAPTER 3

Gordon – The pre war years

In the summer of 1933, a new school was opened at Northern Parade, and on the basis of our address, I was reallocated there. This was a modern school for senior girls and boys, and junior girls and boys. It boasted four grass quadrangles, and glass sliding doors along the length of each classroom, and central heating. The doors between the girls and boys schools were kept permanently locked, but the playgrounds were only separated by railings, so we were able to converse (and throw things). My school life blossomed at Northern Parade junior school. Firstly I was trialled for the school football team, and played regularly at right full back, and was made Captain of the team. We wore orange and black quartered shirts, black shorts, and black socks with orange tops. We were a very elegant team! John Hewinson of whom you will hear much more later, was in the team at right half. I can't remember how well we did that first season, but I don't think we won anything. We had a marked out practice cricket pitch in the playground, and a master who had represented Hampshire as coach. I opened the batting for the school, and was also the cricket captain. It was during this season, that I was chosen to play cricket for Portsmouth junior schools, at Alexandra Park. I was also made a prefect when the school first opened, and was elected by the other prefects as Head Prefect and Captain of the school.

Because I was in the school football team, we frequently got offered through the school, complimentary tickets to Fratton Park, to watch Pompey play. Boys in those days were allowed to sit on the wall on the touch line, in front of the north stand, so we had an uninterrupted view of the game. On Saturday night the Football Mail was delivered, and the highlight was to see if your name appeared in the school results section. Pompey lost 2-1 to Manchester City in the 1934 cup final, but were to do much better in 1939 against Wolves, winning 4-1. Then they held the FA cup because of the war until 1945, the longest time any team has held it. During the 1930's Pompey were a solid rather than a team of internationals. This was to come in the late 1940's post war. Being a footballer in the 1930's, meant you played with a leather lace up ball, which became like a lead balloon in wet conditions. We used leather studs in our leather boots, which came out regularly in heavy conditions. You could then buy replacement leather studs from the shoe repair shop, and you had to hammer these into your boots, using a metal 'foot'. These were available in most homes, as they were used for fitting new rubber soles and heels, and steel tips (available in Woolworths) to day shoes, to prolong wear. We didn't have any Dubbin, so mum used to give me goose grease to rub into the leather boots, to help preserve them, and to prevent the leather cracking. How the poor lived!, but most people were the same, and we accepted it all as normal.

As boys we had respect for our teachers (they had a cane which they were prepared to use) and the police. Our tangles with the 'Bobby' on his bike, usually revolved around bunking into events (parks and cinemas), for which you were supposed to pay, trespassing in fields and up trees where you weren't supposed to be, and scrumping apples from trees in private gardens. We always knew however that if caught, the thing most likely to happen was a cuff round the ear, or to be reported back to your parents or school. As we never gave our real names however this rarely occurred.

We got our first radio when I was about 11. A friend in Hartley road where we lived, made it for us. It consisted of a wooden box with 2 dials on the front for tuning, and it made a whining sound when you were off the station. The speaker which sat on top of the box, was a large bakelite horn. We eventually bought a commercial radio,-a Bush-from a radio shop in 1936, and we thought we were proper posh. .

We did go to Saturday afternoon matinees at the local cinema (The Empire). These small cinemas which ran children's programmes, were affectionately known as bug hutches, and charged 3d downstairs and 4d in the balcony. Upstairs was favourite, as you could throw orange peel, apple cores, or anything solid on to the unfortunates below. They were also very noisy affairs, and I can remember many occasions when the cinema manager came up, and threatened to stop the show, if we did not be quiet and stop throwing things. This never happened I am sure, because he was anxious to get the programme over, and get rid of us as soon as possible. Most of the films were of cowboys and Indians, or consisted of fighting on railway tracks or the top of trains, films which lent themselves to lots of shouting, cheering, or booing. Present day children don't know what they have missed.

In 1933 while we were living at 24 Hartley Rd, Pat got married to Fred. I was always very fond of Fred, and I seemed to know him better than my brother Reg., probably because I saw a lot of Fred., when he visited to be with Pat. Not long after this the family moved from 24 Hartley Rd., a council house, which we had occupied since Dad left the Army in 1926, to a rented house No 27 on the other side of the road. No 27 was a much nicer house and garden, but I never really knew at the time why we had to move up market. At No 24 we had kept chickens and had raspberry, red currant, and black currant bushes. At No 27 we had a lawn, a garden shed, and roses, and some Saturday mornings, if I helped by doing odd jobs in the garden, I was rewarded with a cream cake bought from the baker, when he delivered the bread in his horse and cart.

Although this was a good year for me in many ways, academically it was disastrous. I had been expected to do well at my 11 plus exam., but in the event, I failed to get a place at the Secondary School, and so in September 1934, I went on to the Northern Parade senior boys school. My teacher here was a Mr.H.L.Monckom, who often took a number of the boys in his class, in his car, to visit places of interest in the surrounding countryside. I shudder to think what the pundits would make of that today, but to us it was a day out, and a car drive. During this academic year, I took the entrance exam for a place at the Junior Technical School, (the junior part of the Municipal College), which I passed easily, and took up my place there in September 1935. The school was divided into 4 years and 4 houses viz.Knights, Lords, Monarchs and Nobles, usually referred to as K.L.M.and N. and whose colours were respectively yellow, green, red and black. Whereas at Northern Parade school we were first years, and too young to break into school sports, at the JTS we played our sport in years, and between houses, so I was able to play football and cricket, for the whole three years I was there, developing into a useful opening bat and fast/medium bowler, and playing right back/centre half at football.

The school was very progressive. All the masters were academically well qualified (mostly science and maths), and we had our own science, woodworking, and metalworking laboratories. Also the masters could offer between them specialist gifts in writing, music, both choral and orchestral, and painting. These talents were exploited in the excellent annual concerts they produced, writing the libretto, the music, painting the scenery, and in the stage production. During my three years they produced 'The Bey of Barbary' in 1935, 'Scares of State' in 1936, and 'Greenwood Breeze in 1937. I still have some of the music, and still remember some of the songs (as Muriel will confirm). All parts in the school plays were performed by the boys, so it inevitably fell to some of the boys to play the part of girls. Because I was a member of the Garrison Church choir, and had a fairly good voice, I was persuaded to be in all these plays dressed as a girl. The costumes were excellent, and were the product of our teacher's wives, assisted by our mothers. These three years were to be the last of my full time education, and I look back on them with much satisfaction, and pleasure.

As a boy I had always enjoyed singing, and my friend John Hewinson introduced me to the Hilsea Garrison church choir. The church no longer exists, as it was destroyed many years after the war, and replaced by a large housing estate. The night I joined the choir I was persuaded by John and some of the older boys, (in a sort of initiation ceremony), to climb on to the church roof. Unfortunately we were caught by the Minister, whose words to me were 'and who are you?' When I explained I was a new choir member, he seemed less than impressed. As time passed John and I became the oldest boys and ruled the younger ones. Our games of running football outside the church, when we took on the rest of the choir, (about 10 boys) and always won, were a combination of skill and strategy, with just a little bit of shoulder charging (allowed in those days).

While we were in the choir, John and I were confirmed by the Bishop of Portsmouth, and were allowed to be the first to the altar rail, for Holy Communion. John and I became increasingly close, and during one holiday, he and I visited Pat and Fred in their married Quarters in Netley Hospital, where Fred, then a sergeant in the RAMC, was stationed. His visit must have impressed John greatly, so much so that in 1938, when he was 15, he joined the army as an apprentice, even though as a younger boy he had been a naval cadet at Whale Island (HMS Excellent a naval gunnery school) in Portsmouth. This enforced separation hardly affected our friendship, and we always got together when he came home on leave. You will be hearing more of John later. As time passed I stayed in the choir and became Head Boy (Fig.7), and after my voice broke, for a short time I transferred to the men's section, as an Alto, but the war had overtaken our lives, and I left the choir early in 1940.

I was not the only member of our family to enjoy singing. My mother used to sing around the house, and was noted for putting her own words, to music she heard on the wireless, and also to singing songs she learnt as a girl at school. I heard them so often that I learnt them by heart, and still remember many of them to this day. One about a black dolly called topsy, Muriel learned from me, and sang it to Neil and Rosemary when they were young. I have included the ones I can remember, in an appendix at the end of this narrative.

CHAPTER 4

Muriel-the pre war years

L ooking back, despite all the ups and downs, I had a happy childhood. My other close friend was Beryl Green, who lived in a pub named the "Coburg Arms" in Coburg St. not far away. I met her when I was in the choir, as she went to a different school in Fratton. I went to her home sometimes for tea on Sundays, and we always had tinned cherries. Next door to Beryl lived three boys, and their lovely Alsatian dog called beauty. She suffered us children patiently when we tried to climb on her back.

After my cousin stopped teaching me the piano, Nana and Pops sent me to a music teacher when I was about 10 years old, and I was very proud of my leather music case with my initials on it. She was a good teacher and I was glad I was a reasonable pupil, as she would tap pupils on the knuckles when they played wrong notes. She had trained at Trinity College and was strict. I practised scales on my grandparents piano in the front room, which was very cold in the winter. My hands would get frozen, and Pops would bring in a small Valor oil stove, so I could warm my hands. Often Pops would come into the room to listen to me playing. My hands and feet were often cold and I got chilblains on my fingers, and worst of all, on my ankles, and round the back of my legs, which would drive me mad with the itching, especially at school. Every winter was the same, so I suppose my circulation was poor, and with the lack of heating in the house, it was very uncomfortable. The trouble was that I would sit too close to the fire in the kitchen, which was not good. Nana asked one of her friends if she knew what to do about chilblains. The silly woman told her to put plain washing soda on them. It did stop the itching, but left me with red marks all over my feet and legs. They still appear even now, and when doctors ask me how they got there, I have to explain about Nana's friend. At school we played netball and other ball games, and I skipped, and I walked to and from school. I was always on the move, so I should have had good circulation. I have always been a chilly mortal, so central heating now is lovely.

One day Beryl and I were walking between our homes, when a man on a bicycle, and in a raincoat spoke to us. We ran to her house like the wind we were so scared, but when two plainclothes policemen came to the house to question me, I think I was even more scared of them. But it was all part of growing up.

About the time my father remarried, my mother got in touch with my grandparents, so I was able to see her again. In 1934 someone must have taken me to my mother's flat, and there I found a fair haired child sitting in a high chair. It was of course my half sister Greta. After that Mum, and Greta used to come and visit at Nana and Pop's house. Once when the Bartletts were there, Greta saw Mr.Bartlett in his navy uniform, and ran away saying, 'where's that boy has he gone'. She was a bit scared of him, but she was only about 2 years old. Eventually Mum moved to a rented house nearer to us, so I was able to walk round to see her sometimes.

It was there that I met Greta's father Bert. Tombs. He was a steward on the Canadian Pacific liner Empress of Britain, a lovely ship of about 43000 tons. She did a 6 month world cruise every winter, then crossings between Southampton and New York during the summer months, so Dad (as I now called him) wasn't home very much. He brought home many souvenirs from the ship, one of which was a book all about the world cruise. It had many glossy photos, in some of which he was included in his uniform, looking very smart, and carrying a tray of drinks above his head. A lot of famous people travelled on the ship, including Hollywood stars like Mary Pickford, Warner Oland, (Charlie Chan) and Douglas Fairbanks. Greta and I could not find the book when Mum passed away unfortunately.

Eventually Dad was promoted bedroom steward, and he could tell a few tales about the celebrities. The rich and famous would give him generous tips, especially if he had seen some indiscretion. Mum Greta and I went to Southampton, and Dad took us on board his ship. We had never seen anything so luxurious. Fabulous chandeliers, gold fittings, crystal, paintings by famous artists, and every comfort you could think of.

Dad would bring home American magazines, and once brought home for Mum a beautiful evening dress of ice blue chiffon, like Ginger Rogers wore, given to him by a passenger, but Mum had nowhere she could wear it. I think Birdie probably took it, and flogged it. When I was about 12, Mum moved to a bigger rented house in Church Rd., near St. Mary's church, which was a bit nearer to Foster Rd. When Dad came home from one of his 6 month cruises, we met him at the Docks, and brought home by train, a large camphor wood chest from Hong Kong. Mum was delighted and very proud of it. Neil and Micheline now have it in their hall. When Auntie Birdie saw it she immediately wanted one, and asked Bert to bring one home for her. What a cheek! As if Dad had just popped up the road for it. I often wondered if she paid for it, and for its transport. The chest was identical to Mum's, and Birdie kept it on the landing in her Elm Grove flat, which she had moved into when she married Sam, a gunner in the Royal

Marines. When Birdie passed away, Greta acquired the chest, and now has it in her home.

I don't remember Birdie's wedding, so I don't know where it took place. Uncle Sam was very easy going, and Birdie bossed him about. He bought me a bicycle on my 11th. Birthday, and I can remember going to see his family in Slough. He would take me to the dockyard on Navy Days, and took me on board the battleship HMS Hood, on which he was then a crew member. I also went on board the aircraft carrier HMS Courageous, HMS Belfast, HMS Barham, and other ships. I can also remember going aboard a submarine, although I can't recall when, but probably also on Navy Days, when dockyard ships were open to the public. Sometimes I would be at Mum's house for an overnight stay, and Nana, Pops and Birdie would come round when they found out Dad was home, and they would go out for a drink (Dad always had plenty of money for drinks on his home trips), and leave me in charge of Greta asleep upstairs, and with the cat a lovely tabby called 'Toots', named from a child's book. Toots was very amusing, and could jump up and unlatch the back door, and also switch off the lights. The switches were different then, and you would be sitting reading, and the lights would go out. He would also sit on the table with a paper bag on his head. He was quite a character.

Auntie Birdie had a friend called Miss Dinniford, who worked in a cake shop in Southsea. I called her Auntie Dinnie, and she always gave me a lovely Yule log cake every Christmas. I still remember how delicious those cakes were, with lots of chocolate butter icing. I was with Auntie Birdie and Auntie Dinnie, when we went on the ferry to Sandown, in the Isle of Wight, and had tea at an outside café. I wanted jam sandwiches, and took a bite out of one without seeing the wasp in it. The next moment I was spiting out wasp and sandwich all over the place. The wretched wasp buzzed around my mouth, and stung me inside my bottom lip, and my mouth came up like a balloon. Luckily I hadn't been stung on the tongue, or throat, which would have been very dangerous. Auntie Birdie eventually found a chemist open (it was Sunday and all the shops were shut) and he gave me something to put on the sting. When I was about 11, Jackie the dog and Teewee the cat disappeared. They had died of course, but it was kept from me. Then two new black and white cats Spatty and Bimbo appeared. Spatty would come when called in at night, but Bimbo was reluctant, and I would have to go down the garden in the dark to persuade him, which didn't please me, so I rather favoured Spatty (so called because he had an extra claw on two of his feet.)

Nana loved the cinema, and took me with her sometimes. She also took me to the Coliseum, a variety and music theatre a few times, where I saw Max Miller and Florrie Ford among others. Auntie Birdie also took me to the cinema to see musicals, and to the Kings Theatre, where I saw Jack Buchanan and Elsie Randolph. Two of my friends belonged to a dance group, and one of them could tap dance on her toes. I watched their concerts in Irene Selwood's Dance Troupe (well known in Portsmouth) in halls, and on the sea front.

I kept very busy, as I belonged to Lake Rd Baptist church children's choir, with Barbara, and Beryl. We really loved it, so with homework, piano and choir practice, and visits to friends, there was plenty to do. We didn't go on holidays because we couldn't afford them, and only had a months school holiday in summer, plus two weeks at Christmas, one week at Easter and one day for half term (a far cry from today's lavish holiday routine), but I had a happy time. Barbara, Beryl, and I, had a lot of fun in the Baptist church choir, which I had joined when I was 10. It consisted of about 50 boys and girls, and we had a choirmaster, and a dancing teacher.

Like most boys, ours were terrors, and during practices, used itching powder and sneezing powder, which could be bought cheaply in those days. In May 1935 we went to London to do a concert in a hall near St Paul's, and in June we took part in a competition and concert in the Crystal Palace, and a Christmas concert at the church. The choir belonged jointly to the Baptist church, and to the Temperance Society (Band of Hope), which was a very strong movement in those days. I don't think any of us belonged to the church, and our families certainly didn't belong to the Temperance Society!. We three girls were always among the dancers, especially at the Christmas concert.

It was very exciting for us to go by train to London, to the Crystal Palace, which was unfortunately burned down the very next year 1936. It was entirely made of glass with palms, ponds, statues and fountains, and the concert hall was huge with an enormous organ. In the grounds there was a large boating lake, where we hired boats, messing about in them with 'kiss me quick' hats on. It was a wonder we didn't all fall in. Around the lake were trees and bushes, and between them were huge stone statues of mammoths, dinosaurs etc. There was also a funfair with different free rides, like the chair-a-plane (a roundabout with boats hanging from the top)

The day consisted firstly of taking part in our section of the competition, prior to which we were not allowed to eat biscuits or sweets, only sandwiches and fruit. After we had been allowed to look around, all the choirs joined together to give a joint concert, after which we could eat what we liked. Choirs of all ages came from all over the country, and a Welsh choir usually won. One year we came third. In 1936 and 1937, after the destruction of the Crystal Palace, the competition took place at the Alexandra Palace. The choir had other outings, and in August we went to Littlehampton, not to sing, but to have fun on the beach. Once a year the Band of Hope held a demonstration, which our choir joined. We walked from St. Mary's church to Alexandra Park, carrying our banners, and in fancy dress, with the floats and bicycles also dressed up. (Although I didn't know it at the time, Gordon who lived close to the park and used it regularly, refused to pay the entrance fee to get in the park on these occasions, and 'bunked in' through the railings.)

When Mum lived in Stamford St, she had to have all her teeth out, because she had some sort of gum disease. It was done at home in her bedroom (how awful), and I had to stay downstairs out of the way with Greta. How she managed with no one to help her I can't imagine-I suppose there was a nurse there. It couldn't happen today in the NHS, she would have been hospitalised. But people in those days didn't visit the dentist , doctor, or optician on a regular basis because you had to pay for these visits then, and they couldn't afford it. I was scared of the dentist, whose treatment then was very different from today. I remember on one occasion Nana took me to the dentist, but I wouldn't go in, and ran home, but that was before I had my second teeth. I also remember Nana taking me to the eye dept at the hospital, having drops put in my eyes, and sitting on long wooden forms in a big room before the optician would see you. Everything was very primitive compared to today.

Christmas was a very nice time. On Christmas eve Nana and I would go shopping, and I would buy my presents in Woolworths, where everything cost 6d or less. Then we would go to the local market to buy a chicken for Christmas dinner, nuts, tangerine oranges, fruit and vegetables. Pops would pluck the chicken, and use a taper to singe off the feathers, before Nana prepared it for cooking the next day. On Christmas day I had to stay in bed to keep out of Nana's way. When I got up I was given a bowl of water to wash in the front room, where Pops had lit a fire. Then I would look at my presents—the party dress which had been hanging on the wardrobe, a stocking with nuts, and an orange, and two large Annuals, the Schoolgirls Own and the School Friend. I had these same weekly comics. Nana said I always had my nose stuck in a book Sometimes for tea we had a small iced cake, and in the evening Nana and Pops had friends round. Pops had a barrel of beer, Nana had something stronger, and I had a big stone jar of lemonade. I played the piano for everyone to sing along to.

One year Auntie Birdie had a family gathering in her flat after Christmas, when two of Uncles Sam's friends joined them, and they played gramophone records. One of these men was Jack Maltby, a Marine musician, and the other one was Jack Nash, a Marine reservist. Jack Nash was no relation, but Greta and I called him Uncle Jack. He lived with his wife Ivy in Steyning Sussex, and worked as the school caretaker at Steyning Grammar school. Occasionally Auntie Birdie took me to the Marine barracks at Eastney on Sunday mornings, to the church parade, which were a regular feature of services life. We met Uncle Sam after the parade, and went to a pub called the Shell House opposite the barracks, and sat in he garden where there were lots of sea shells, and patterned plates embedded in the walls.

I was very lucky to go to lots of Christmas parties. At Christmas time 1934 and 1935, I stayed at Auntie Dinnie's flat overnight, with my cousins Brenda and Joan, so that I could go to a big party at the army drill hall. My father was there with Uncle Fred, who had been a drum major in the army, and he was dressed in a leopard skin, and banging a big drum. Father Christmas arrived in a sleigh with all the presents on it, and the children watched from the balcony around the hall. The room was in darkness except for the lights on the sleigh, and some carried by the band and procession.

Then we would all go into a large room, where there was a large tree, around which Father Christmas had put all the presents for distribution to the children. I remember having silver shoes, and a party dress for this event. In 1935 I also went to a party at the Masonic hall. Uncle Fred who was a Mason got me the invitation, but I had a nasty cold coming, and as none of my friends were there, I didn't enjoy it very much.

In 1936 and 1937 Uncle Sam took me to Christmas parties for naval children at Whale Island (HMS Excellent), the naval gunnery school. The sailors helped with all the games at these parties, and we had lots of fun. A few of my friends also held Christmas parties at their homes. Nana and Pops were very good, and allowed me to have a party in their garden in 1936, and several school friends came. Barbara's father belonged to something called the Prince of Wales, and Barbara and I went to their Boxing day dances, at the Esplanade ballroom in 1937 and 1938 The hall had a coloured glass dance floor in squares of red and green, lit from below, so Barbara and I in our first long party dresses, enjoyed that. The main ballroom had a balcony, where the dance band played, and had small areas round it separated by trellis, filled with imitation flowers and tables, where people sat. Barbara's mum and dad were very good, and each took a turn round the dance floor with us, otherwise Barbara and I danced together. We could both dance, so we weren't a nuisance to adults on the floor, but we joined in the Paul Jones sometimes. Auntie Birdie made my long party dresses as Christmas presents, the one in 1937 being pink taffeta with ruching, and the one in 1938 was apple green taffeta, with a sash of pink and mauve plaited velvet. She was very kind, and wanted me to look nice. She also used to curl my hair with curling tongs, which were heated on top of the gas cooker. On a few occasions she caught the top of my ear, which hurt a lot.

Beryl Green's brother Harry took us on the bus to the fair on Ports-down hill at Whitsun. We weren't very clever at the coconut shy, so Harry had to get them for us. Pops would give me a little money to spend on the side shows, and on the rides. Every year on Guy Fawke's night, Pops would give me 6d to spend on fireworks. They were very cheap, and although we didn't have a bonfire, Pops lit the fireworks for me, after the cats had been shut indoors.

At Good Friday and Easter, in 1937 and 1938, some school friends and I, took a bus to the top of Portsdown hill, and after walking over the hill to the villages of Widley and Southwick, we had a picnic. There were about six of us, including the headmaster's nieces. At these walks and picnics I always seemed to have tomato and banana sandwiches, which got a bit soggy, and an apple, and a small bar of chocolate, so even though I got hungry, I did very well. When we got to Southwick we usually sat outside a 'Gales Ales' pub, which was owned by Barbara's aunt, and then we would go picking bluebells in the woods, where there were masses of them. There were also plenty of wild flowers which we could pick in those days, as there were no restrictions like there are today. Monica, one of our group, was always looking for boys to talk to. She was a bit keen on the lads, although I don't remember her being like it with boys at school, perhaps because she was under the watchful eye of her uncle. In those days children were quite safe going into the countryside unaccompanied, not like it is today.

Sometime in 1938 after Mum moved to Church Rd., Dad's father came to live there. I didn't like him very much, as he was a bit grouchy and bossy with Mum, but he lived there until Mum was bombed out during the early part of the war.

CHAPTER 5

Muriel, The early war years

BY September 1938 I was not only doing normal lessons at school, but was also learning shorthand, typing, and tracing. Life had settled into a pattern of living with Nana and Pops, and sometimes staying with Mum and Greta at week ends, from Saturday morning to Sunday afternoon. Mum would take Greta and I to the new cinema the "Troxy", which had opened in Fratton road just before the War. The cinema was very modern and comfortable, with an organ which rose from a pit in the front of the stage. The organist would play all the latest popular tunes, and the words were projected on the screen, so that the audience could sing along. We all loved it. I remember the first film we saw was 'Queen of Hearts', starring Gracie Fields. We also saw Deanna Durbin in her first film, 'Three Smart Girls', and she became my idol. All the young girls wanted to be like her. (It was very touching when Gordon and I visited Ann Frank's house in Amsterdam, when we were on holiday in the 1990's, as there was a picture of Deanna Durbin, cut from a magazine, stuck on the bedroom wall) After the cinema, we would go to the cake shop, and buy a fancy cream gateau for tea, before I went back to Nana and Pop's house. Pops took on a job as a night watchman at the 'Troxy', and had a hut at the back of the cinema, but after a while he left, as I think Auntie Birdie worried about him being there all night on his own, at his age. Barbara and I were still great friends, but we no longer played with the toys we used, when we were younger. I saw a lot of Beryl too, and was fortunate in keeping my old friends.

In September 1938 before the new school term started, Mum, Greta, Barbara, and I, all went for a short holiday, to stay with Auntie Ivy and Uncle Jack, in Steyning. At that time Uncle Jack was the caretaker at Steyning Grammar school, a very old boarding school for boys, and he showed us round the school. He was also a Royal Marine reservist, and his way of life was about to be changed. We all loved Steyning as it was lovely countryside, and Auntie Ivy's house was right at the foot of the Downs. They had a long garden, with chickens, and grew their own vegetables, and the garden gate led on to the road leading up to the Downs. I remember Auntie Ivy getting hold of one of the chickens, and when I asked what she was going to do, she said, wring its neck for Sunday dinner. I soon hopped round the corner of the house, I just couldn't watch. Auntie Ivy was a proper country woman and I was a coward. Christmas day was happy as usual with all the family together, and Greta's Dad acting as barman, and thoroughly enjoying it.

In August 1939 Mum, Auntie Birdie, Greta my friend Barbara and I, went to stay in Steyning, Sussex, again, with Auntie Ivy and Uncle Jack. They had a lovely black spaniel called Trixie, who we were very fond of. We had a lovely week in the sunshine, and then had to return home. At the end of August, Mum, Greta, Auntie Birdie and I were again visiting Auntie Ivy's house, and on 31st August I spent my 14th. Birthday there. We were listening to the radio on 3rd. September, when Neville Chamberlain, our Prime Minister, made the speech which worried us all. He said he had sent an ultimatum to Hitler to leave Poland, but as he had not done so, Britain had declared war on Germany. Needless to say

Auntie Birdie and Auntie Ivy were very upset, as their husbands had already been recalled to the Royal Marines, and they knew they would be fighting a war very soon. Greta's Dad was away on the 'Empress of Britain' in Canada. We later learned that his ship was delayed in Canada, and eventually when he returned to Portsmouth, he told us that he had to return to England in a merchant ship, in an Atlantic convoy

In the first few months of the war, not a great deal changed, and I was still at school with my friends. When Greta's Dad got home, he had to report to the employment exchange, but as he was not the right age for the services, he managed to get a job as a steward, in the RAOC Officers mess at Hilsea, and being the sort of work he was used to, he enjoyed it . Mum and Greta and I lived in Mum's house in Church Rd., except when I was with Nana and Pops in Foster Rd.

CHAPTER 6

Muriel, The war years

In 1940 I was at home with Nana and Pops, when we experienced an air raid for the first time. It was a lovely hot summer day, and I was in the garden, and looking up I counted 17 bombers in the sky. Nana came into the garden and looked quite scared, but Pops carried on gardening. In the evening we went to see where the bombs had come down in Kingston Rd., and at the Princes cinema in Lake Rd. The air raids had really started

1939 and early 1940 was known as the phoney war, but in the middle of 1940, the Battle of Britain started. It was a lovely summer with clear blue skies, showing the trails of the aircraft fighting. Mum, Greta, and I hid under the stairs for most of the time, while the aerial dog fights were going on overhead, as we found it safer to keep way from the inevitable falling shrapnel. You had to be careful. Most of the bombing at this time was on London, but we did have a few bombs on Portsmouth, and with the novelty of it, we naturally went to see the damage caused. Little did we know how much more damage was to come, and our involvement in it. After Hitler lost the Battle of Britain, night bombing started in the latter part of 1940.

On the Monday evening after Christmas 1940, I got home to change into my slacks, woollies etc. I was just about to open the kitchen door, when there was a tremendous bang, and the door flew back open into my hand. We didn't know exactly what it was, but we suspected a stick of bombs, and the next morning on the way to work along the Dockyard wall, we saw a row of small terrace houses, had been very badly damaged. All their doors and windows had gone, and wallpaper, curtains and Christmas decorations, were littering the street. We could see the damage had to have been caused by something very big, and there was talk of a plane and its load of bombs having crashed there.

On January 10th 1941 Portsmouth had one of its heaviest attacks, with 3 separate raids lasting from early evening, until about 6.am. the next morning. On this Thursday evening, Barbara and I were hurrying home from the wine merchants Smeed & Smeed, where we worked, sheltering under the shop awnings as we went. I hurried indoors as the air raid had already started, and didn't have time to eat much, before diving into our neighbour's Anderson, shelter in their garden, which Mr.and Mrs.Ross had kindly offered to share with us. We sat and shivered, very much afraid, from 6.pm until about 11 pm when the bombing eased. When we emerged from the shelter, we found Nana and Pop's house on fire upstairs. The bedrooms, especially mine were burning, and downstairs, part of the front of the house was damaged. Pop's birdcages were smashed on the kitchen table, all the birds were dead, and the two cats nowhere to be seen. We never saw them again, so they were either killed or ran off in fright. After helping the men on the roof, (probably air raid wardens) trying to put the fires out, poor Pops collapsed on the floor. He was soaked to the skin, and we thought he was dead, but eventually he recovered.

I was so worried about Mum and Greta, that I ran to look for them in their house in Church Rd. I kept calling her, and was so relieved when Mum answered me. Her house had no front door, and her bedding was wrapped around the doorway and bedroom windows. Luckily they had been in the street shelter. The shop opposite, which was normally used by 17 air raid wardens, was empty that night, and I didn't see any of them. The whole road was a mess. At the end of Mum's road in St.Mary's churchyard, there was a large barrage balloon, manned by the RAF. I could see the balloon on fire, and servicemen trying to put it out. Then I heard Pops calling me. He had sent Mr. Ross (our neighbour) to look for me, but as he hadn't appeared, I think he had gone back to his wife in the shelter. The whole area was devastated, fires everywhere, the whole of Portsmouth seemed to be alight. Everywhere was a mess, like a battlefield, with bodies, household goods and glass underfoot. I didn't know what I was walking on, as the only light was from the fires. There was now no electricity, and so the air raid sirens could not sound for the second raid at about midnight. Mum, Greta, and Dad's father who was staying with Mum, went back to their street shelter, and I went back with Pop's to the Ross's Anderson shelter. Eventually there was a break in the bombing, and Pops Nana and I went out to try to do something in the house. It is all a bit of a blur now, but I remember between the second and third raids, Pops asked me to act as a messenger, and I ran to some shelters to tell people their houses were on fire. I don't remember how, but we managed to get some water to drink, although many water mains were broken, and there was a shortage of water for fire fighting, and stirrup pumps. We thought the raids had finished, but about 2 am they started again, and finally ended at about 6am. Fortunately our houses did not get bombed again during the second and third raids, but we learned later that one of Dad's sisters had been in a shelter which received a direct hit, and she, and three of her children were killed .

Although the upstairs of Nana and Pops house was totally burned out, the downstairs was just habitable, and the kitchen and middle room were usable. This was fortunate, as Nana now had to do all the cooking for Mum and Greta, as well as Nana, Pops and me. What happened in the following days is now only a blur, but I do remember we all had our meals together at Nana and Pops house, and Nana, Pops and I slept on the floor downstairs. I did stay with Auntie Birdie in her flat in Elm Grove for a while, but her flat was also bombed in an air raid on March 10th, so she also had to go to Nana and Pops house for her meals. Auntie Birdie soon recognised that Nana and Pops were too old to carry on living like this, so in April, she arranged for all three of them to be evacuated to Steyning, Auntie Birdie living with Auntie Ivy, and Nana and Pops living in rooms in a house opposite, owned by a Mr.and Mrs.Francis.

I now had to move in with Mum and Greta. Mum had found a damaged property nearby, with an Anderson shelter, the residents having moved away from the area. Mum, Greta and I, together with our tabby cat named Toots, slept every night in the Anderson shelter. I've no idea where we washed, or cleaned our clothes. Then on April 21st.while we were in a street shelter, a land mine landed on the house opposite to our temporary accommodation, and shook our street shelter. A young girl standing just outside the shelter, was blown into the shelter by the blast and killed . The parachute of the land mine landed in a tree in our front garden, and it was probably this, and the fact that Dad could not get back to Portsmouth (and didn't want to), that made up Mum's mind, that we could not go on any longer living like this. Greta's Dad had by now been transferred in his civilian job in the RAOC Officers mess at Hilsea, to the RA Officers mess at Leicester. Mum felt that living in a billet in Leicester, would be preferable to living with two children in an Anderson shelter, so in May we moved to Leicester, and were billeted with a Major Warr-Diamond, and his wife.

This was a very unhappy period. The Major's wife, even though she was being paid for our billet, made it clear we were there on sufferance, and not wanted, and she made things as unpleasant and uncomfortable as possible, while we were there. She treated us as inferiors, for example bringing the potatoes for lunch to us in a saucepan, and which we had to eat in the bedroom. Because Bert was a civilian, he was unable to improve the situation. While I was living in Leicester I developed a bad back rash, for which Mum had to take me to the doctor for treatment. The doctor said this was a nervous complaint, and I believe it was caused by all the trauma I had suffered, during the bombing in Portsmouth. As the situation deteriorated, and there was no possibly of changing billets, Mum decided the situation was intolerable, and in September, she arranged for us also to go to Steyning, and stay with Auntie Ivy The family were all together at last, but I remember that as Mum was the best cook, she did the cooking for all of us.

Steyning was in a valley, and Auntie Ivy's house, where we were staying, was at the bottom of a country road, that climbed a hill leading eventually to Chanctonbury Ring (a stand of trees at the top). Pops was in his element here with the countryside and the animals, and I would often walk partly up the hill with him, followed by Auntie Ivy's cat. I did make friends with a local girl named Pat O'Connor, but I missed my old friends Barbara and Beryl. In 1942 before the abortive attempt on Dieppe, some Canadian soldiers were camped at the top of the hill prior to the assault. Although I remember they were a rough lot, they were never any trouble to the local residents, and they often came to collect water from them.

Jobs were impossible to find in Steyning, and Mum decided in 1943 as I approached 18, that we must move back to Portsmouth where the bombing had now decreased, and Mum found a house in St Chads Ave. North End. While we were here we had a few air raid warnings, and Mum and I would shelter under the stairs. At this time Greta stayed in Steyning as an evacuee. The first job I got was as a ledger clerk at the Danish Bacon Co., and I hated it so much, I left after a week. Smeed & Smeed the wine merchants where I had worked before, had moved into new premises after being bombed out, and I managed to obtain a job there as a typist, and where I was reunited with my old friend Barbara. In August 1943 I became 18, and I had to find a wartime job or join the Services. At the time I wanted to go into the RAF, but I was persuaded not to. Through a friend of Mum's I obtained a Dock-yard related job as a shorthand typist at Swanmore, an engine spares and equipment Depot, which had been evacuated from the Engineering Dept in the Dockyard. The depot was some 15 miles north of Portsmouth, and employed a mix of locally entered staff, and staff evacuated from the Dockyard.

The office opened at 7.30am, so the dockyard staff of whom I was one, had a very early morning start, travelling to Swanmore. The form of travel varied, and at different periods was undertaken by Naval lorry, commercial bus services (Southdown from Portsmouth to Fareham and then Hants and Dorset to Swan-more) and eventually by contract coaches. Travelling time varied from $3/_4$ hour to $1^1/_2$ hours, depending on the form of transport. The female staff were not required to work at night, so I spent every evening from about 7 o'clock, at home. While I was travel-ling to and from Swanmore, I can remember the country lanes which we had to travel along being crowded with troops, lorries, and tanks, just prior to the invasion in June 1944.

In August 1943, just after we had moved back to Portsmouth and I was working at Swanmore I developed a poisonous abscess on my neck, which had to be removed at the Royal Hospital. I was in hospital for about a week, and after I came out, my father appeared at our house and said he had heard about my illness, and asked after my health. I believe my mother gave him a "right earful", pointing out that he had made no attempt to find out how I was during all the bombing raids. Greta's father Bert was eventually called up, and left his Officers Mess civilian job, and was drafted as a Private to an AA Battery in the London area. The gunfire seriously affected his hearing, and because of this he was sent to hospital, and eventually demobbed. He then returned to live with us at St. Chad's Ave. and obtained a job as a steward on the cross channel ferry boats, operating from Southampton to Jersey. Having been demobbed from the army he returned to the sea where he was happiest, but could not get back to the CPR ships on which he had previously served.)

A draughtsman named Gordon had joined at Swanmore early in 1944, but was transferred to HQ in Bath early in 1945. During the time we spent together at Swanmore, our friendship blossomed, and we got engaged in 1945. I remained at Swanmore for a time after Gordon left, but eventually after some disagreement with the Officer in Charge, I transferred back to the Engineering Dept typing pool in the dockyard. I was very happy here, and made many new friends, and eventually became assistant supervisor. Because Gordon had transferred temporarily to the Customs and Excise Dept. at Southampton in 1947 he was living at home at Southsea at the time. After 2 years (quite normal for an engagement in those days), Gordon and I were married at St Marks Church in September 1947. We spent our honeymoon in Jersey in the Channel Islands, and travelled on the ship on which Bert was now serving as a steward. He managed to get us a cabin berth for the trip, rather than the deck accommodation Gordon had been able to book. Jersey was just recovering from the war, but we enjoyed our stay at a refurbished hotel called "Swansons". As a wedding present, Bert managed to get us a decorated tea service in Jersey, something which was unobtainable in England at the time.

After a year at Southampton, Gordon was appointed to a job in Portsmouth Dockyard, and during this time I remained at my job in the typing pool with my new friends, until Gordon appointed to Plymouth in1950, after passing the Civil Service Executive exam. I eventually joined him in Plymouth in1951.

CHAPTER 7

Gordon, The war years

In 1938 at the Junior Technical School, I took the national Civil
Service examination for entry to the Royal Dockyards, as an
engineer apprentice. I passed easily and was appointed to
Portsmouth Dockyard in October. Part of the attraction of these
apprenticeships, which were fiercely contested throughout the
country, was the opportunity to attend the Royal Dockyard
School (later the Royal Dockyard Technical College) on a part
time basis over a period of 4 years. The classes for apprentices of
all trades were held in the afternoon and evenings, and the standard was fully competitive up to University entrance. Pupils
were split between the upper and lower schools, the top achiev-
ers at the end of each year going forward to the next 'Year'. The
fourth year consisted of a very small group of the best academically, many of whom went on to University. I managed to
achieve two years in the upper school and one year in the lower
school.

During my third year 1940/41, the school was bombed out
like so much of the dockyard, and we continued our interrupted
education in a private school in Portsmouth, from which the
pupils had been evacuated. I also started a correspondence course
for the AMIMech.E qualification at this time, but with the continuous bombing, Home Guard and fire watching duties, it was

never completed. It was to be a further 47 years before I eventually achieved my degree.

By 1938 the war clouds were gathering, and it soon became apparent that Chamberlain's attempt to secure peace with Hitler would come to nothing. It did however give us a whole year to make our preparations for war, which turned out to be invaluable. In September 1939 war was declared, and preparations started in earnest. Children were evacuated to the countryside, blackout material was required to be put over all doors and windows to ensure no light shone out in the total blackout, enforced by the ARP wardens, and strips of sticky paper were stuck over windows to prevent flying glass in the event of bomb blast. Identity cards were issued to all civilians, and all signposts and means of identifying places and localities, were removed. From early on in the war gas masks were issued to all civilians including children, and we had to carry them everywhere in a cardboard box with a shoulder strap. I later had a service gas mask issued. There was even a song which was broadcast, reminding people to carry them, but as the war progressed, it was noticeable that more and more people were not bothering to carry them To-gether with some friends, I went to the Royal Hospital in Portsmouth, to paint the outside windows with blue paint, as it was decided that blackout curtains were unsatisfactory. The nurses were all very friendly, and kept us well supplied with food and hot drinks.

The end of 1939 and the start of 1940 was a complete anticlimax. It was a very cold winter when even the sea froze, but we mostly went about our business as normal, although food rationing started in early 1940. In April things changed, and we experienced our first daylight air raids. A stick of 3 bombs demolished the Blue Anchor public house, and the third bomb landed in the next road to Lyndhurst Road where I was living, blowing out the glass in our back windows. Fortunately these early bombs were only 50 pounders, and the raids were classified as nuisance raids. Things were not going well in Europe however, and by May France had collapsed, and the retreat from Dunkirk took place.

Dunkirk was a cataclysmic defeat, as well as a triumphant withdrawal, but the realisation of how close we came to losing the war in May 1940, always comes as a shock.. At this time Lord Halifax was trying to persuade Churchill to sue for peace, but Churchill would have none of it. He said "Nations that go down fighting rise again, but those who surrendered tamely were finished" and later "If this long island history is going to end, let it end when every one of us is choking on his own blood on the ground." Churchill's arguments at the time to his cabinet colleagues were largely emotional, but this really was all we had at the time, and Churchill did eventually convince Parliament that we must fight on, no matter the odds.

The whole point of the Dunkirk saga however, is that it's spirit was unrealistic. AJP Taylor when asked later weren't people worried that Britain was on its own replied, "not at all – ordinary people said we were better off without all those foreigners and we could manage by ourselves" It is hard to understand how fervently patriotic Britain was in 1940. The British really did believe that they were the greatest people in the world, and better than foreigners. But it was only because the British felt this way, that they managed to survive the disasters that 1940 and 1941 brought ie the Blitz, the beginning of starvation by the U boats, and defeat after defeat in the middle east. Churchill was right to warn that wars are not won by evacuations, but in a way, Dunkirk was a victory over the incompetence of the German army, not to have completed the shattering success of the Battle of France, by forcing the BEF to surrender. Although this was obviously a reversal, the bringing back to England of 300,000 troops that could be subsequently redeployed on war service, was a magnificent task, and because the crews of the little boats, went at great risk to themselves, and to their boats. One of those returning to England after Dunkirk was my brother Reg. who was injured, his wounds turned gangrenous, and he spent many months in a hospital in the north of England.

After the miracle of Dunkirk, the threat of invasion became a reality, unknown for a thousand years, and it was with a fierce determination not to submit to the Nazis, and if necessary to fight for our way of life, that the LDV was born in June 1940, after a broadcast appeal by the War Secretary, Anthony Eden. Within 24 hours, 250,000 men had volunteered to join. It was Churchill who disliked the name LDV, (local defence volunteer) and he eventually changed it to Home Guard. By 24th July when it became officially known as the Home Guard, 1.3 million men had joined. People today have no idea of the feelings and sentiments that existed at that time, and it is impossible to convey to those who were not alive then, this mood, (although some do try to do it in hindsight but without success.) Among their earliest duties, was to watch over vulnerable points, such as railway bridges, public buildings, communication centres, power stations etc. against the possibility of German parachutists, thus relieving thousands of regular soldiers of such duties at night. Most Home Guards did of course have daytime civilian duties as well. Our loss of arms and equipment at Dunkirk had been crippling, and at first it was difficult to find enough for our beleaguered army, let alone the Home Guard, so we had to improvise with pikes, pitchforks, and knives lashed on poles, in fact anything that would serve as a weapon. This together with our appearance in badly fitting denim caps and uniforms, helped to provide the lasting impression of the Home Guard, now affectionately known as "Dads Army"

At the time you knew that if the worst came to the worst, you would never survive against highly trained troops, but we constituted a crucial distinction between us, and the European countries, where the invading Germans had encountered no civilian resistance. Things were of course at first chaotic, and typically unmilitary.. The Daily Telegraph reported an incident in a lonely spot, where a Home Guard called 'Halt' to an unidentified figure. 'Halt' said the Home Guard a second time. "I have halted said the man, what do you want me to do now? I don't know said the Home Guard, my orders are to say halt three times and then shoot." Guns, equipment and ammunition gradually became available, and the Home Guard became a huge shield, leaving the army to train to attack, because it was apparent we would have to fight our way back into Europe. Dad's Army helped to pave the way back.

I joined the LDV in August 1940 when I was 17. I joined an Infantry Company responsible for protecting the Guildhall, railway bridges, and important buildings in the city of Portsmouth. On September 10th there was an invasion scare in the south East of the country, and the church bells were rung to summon the Home guard, and other services. The scare turned out to be just that, and in the morning, everyone was stood down to their obvious relief. Later my Company moved to the east coast of Portsmouth, to protect the foreshore. Gradually our training improved, assisted by soldiers who had seen action, but who had for some reason been invalided out of the regular army. We were soon expected to obtain army certificates of proficiency, before being given rank or promotion. I was in due course promoted to corporal on infantry duties. (See Fig.10)

It is not well known that in 1940, when Churchill said 'We will fight them on the beaches,' he had already started to create a top secret army of ordinary men and women, including Home Guards, to spearhead Britain's resistance, if Hitler invaded. They were required to gather vital evidence, and fight from special underground bunkers around the country. They were to be spies and saboteurs, and would have been shot if they had fallen into the hands of the Germans, and a decree by German General Franz Halder discovered after the war confirmed this. Civilians with a good knowledge of their local area, and who were prepared to live rough like poachers, were ideal, and people who needed to travel by virtue of their work, like doctors and bus drivers etc were recruited. These special auxiliary units were trained at a secret location at Coleshill House in Wiltshire, where they were provided with plastic explosives, daggers, garottes, phosphorus hand grenades, mines, booby traps etc. After training they returned to their local areas, and continued their secret training. To give them credence in the community, and with the local Home Guard Battalions, they were given Home Guard uniforms, with special identification flashes. Some 5000 prepared and well armed civilians awaited a German invasion, which fortunately never came. For their own safety as well as for propaganda reasons, these auxiliary units were a closely guarded secret, and I was unaware of their existence. In fact it was 1996 before the Defence Correspondent of The Times, presented an article on these Auxiliers as they were known, and from this a Museum of British Resistance Organisations was created in 1997 at Framlingham airfield, a USAF Base in Suffolk. I received my Defence Medal in 1946, but because of the secrecy surrounding their creation and existence, most Auxiliers did not.

In 1940 every civilian in the country was issued with an Identity Card, in order to obviate spying, and illegal entry to the country. Service men and women always carried a means of identity, and in any case were invariably in uniform. Each change of address had to be notified to the National Registration Officer, and when my card was reissued in 1950, I must have lived in at least 6 homes before that date. My card (which is shown at Fig.8 and Fig.9) was still in use in 1951, and probably stayed in force until Muriel and I sailed to Singapore in 1954.

1940 was a beautiful summer with clear blue skies, and we frequently saw the vapour trails in the sky, as the dogfights took place between the British and German planes. In my diary for that year, I recorded on 15th. September, when it was reported we shot down 175 German planes that day (although these figures were always subject to confirmation, and were usually found to be slightly lower) Certainly we shot down more than the Germans did, and this effectively ended Hitler's plans for the invasion of England. The Battle of Britain officially ended on 31st.October. Daylight bombing had now become too expensive for the Germans, but it did not cease entirely. Both sides now resorted to night bombing, and Portsmouth was to get its share of this. At this time I bought my first car a Morris 8 registration BOR 838, but as I was unable to get the petrol for it, which was rationed, it wasn't long before I had to sell it again without really having made any use of it.

Hitler's reaction to losing the Battle of Britain, was to release his V1 flying bombs, or doodlebugs as they were called. The first of these appeared in late 1940, dropping in London and south east England, causing damage and some casualties. These V1s were like gliders, but had an engine on top of the body, and a payload of explosives. The general assumption at the time was that the V1 fell to earth when the fuel ran out, but in fact they were a little more sophisticated than that. There was a windmill fitted to the nose which logged the mileage. When the pre-set distance was achieved, electrical detonators and a spring loaded trip locked the elevators into a dive position. This attitude exposed the fuel pipe above the now low fuel level, thereby cutting the engine, and producing the well known silence before crashing. These bombs were not intended for specific targets, but acted as a terror weapon to create damage, and affect morale. Sometimes Spitfire planes attempted to "flip" the wings of the V1, to send them crashing to the ground before they could reach London. The last V1 bomb fell on Britain on 22nd. March 1945.

At the beginning of 1941, night bombing increased. Portsmouth had two major raids lasting all night on January 10th., and March 10th. On the first occasion, the raid started early in the evening, and went on till about 11 o'clock A second raid started about 1o'clock, and lasted till 3 o'clock, and a final raid started at about 5 o'clock, and lasted until it was getting light. This was to be the pattern of numerous raids on Portsmouth for a long time to come. My family were very lucky on these raids, and suffered mostly only incon-venience. Muriel suffered badly, as she has already outlined in her notes in a previous chapter. The noise on these raids was deafen-ing, as we had to contend not only with bombs, but falling build-ings, and gunfire. At this time mobile AA guns were employed in the streets, as well as in batteries. After the raids there was no water, and no electricity, for days in various parts of the city, and the light from the thousands of incendiary bomb fires lit up the night sky. The ARP wardens and householders were provided with buckets, stirrup pumps, and sandbags, to try prevent the fires from taking hold in individual households, as the Fire Brigade was employed on the major fires. Landmines were mines on sticks about 6 feet long. As soon as the stick touched the ground, the mines exploded above ground, and this considerably widened the area of damage. These mines were responsible for some quite extraordinary damage, and often affected people and places some distance away, while leaving people and buildings close to the land-mine unscathed.

Apart from these heavies, we had lesser raids almost every night for months It was quite normal to come home from work about 5 o'clock, have tea, and then go to the air raid shelter for the night . We went back into the house in the morning, to dress ready for work the next day. These air raid shelters, called Anderson Shel-ters which were issued to anyone who wanted one, and was pre-pared to pay for it, were like small Nissen huts, made of corru-gated iron sunk into the ground, and covered with earth and sandbags. They contained 4 bunk beds, and you took your food and drink and bedding in with you. They would not have sur-vived a direct or near direct hit, but they offered some protection from blast and shrapnel, and gave a measure of confidence you did not feel in the house. Nevertheless as the war progressed, people became blasé about the bombing, and often stayed in bed, feeling as soldiers did in the fighting zones, that if a bullet had your name on it, that was it, so also if a bomb had your name on it, you couldn't avoid it anyway, so why not try to get a good night's rest in bed.

My apprenticeship, which I had started in October 1938 in the Engineering Dept workshops in the Dockyard, consisted of learning and practising the use of hand tools in the first year, and operating various machines like lathes, milling and shaping machines, in the second year. At the end of each year we were required to pass a trade test, before passing to the next stage. In the third year we were instructed on the refitting of internal combustion, and steam engines, and turbines, and repair of ship fittings, which could be removed from ships to the workshops. During the apprenticeship we attended trade lectures in house, and were required to attend the Dockyard School as I have mentioned earlier.

It was during 1941, that there was a huge daylight raid on the Dockyard. There we had brick and concrete shelters, and we went into them only when there was a 'red' alert, signifying that the bombers were in the immediate vicinity, thus preventing lost time on important ship work. During this raid, a 500 pound bomb was dropped, right outside the shelter I was in. The earth heaved, the walls cracked and moved, and the shelter was filled with dust and small debris. After the all clear sounded, we went to leave the shelter, and found a huge bomb crater right outside one of the door, preventing us from leaving that way. 20 or 30 feet closer, and this biography would not be written, and many of you reading it, would not be here. My mother had been away that day visiting friends, and rushed back when she heard that the dockyard had been bombed.

Reg my brother came home on leave in 1941, but after only a few days went back to barracks. He contended that being bombed, and not being able to hit back, was more frightening than action in the field, where you could move about and be active, to take your mind off the action. This was a period of sadness for my sister Dorothy also. Her husband Andy, whom she had married just before the war started, was killed on HMS Achates, which was bombed and sunk on the Russian convoys. Dorothy was left with two young boys, Sean and Kerry. Dorothy took refuge in poetry at this stage, and I still have some of her writings. Pat my sister, and Fred (an army friend of Reg) were married in 1933, and Shirley was born in 1934, and Michael in 1937. In 1938 Fred was posted to Hong Kong, and Pat eventually joined him there.

Before the Japanese invaded Hong Kong, Pat and the children were evacuated to Australia, and remained there for the rest of the war, coming home to Portsmouth in 1945. Hong Kong fell on Xmas Day 1941. Fred was captured by the Japanese at the Military Hospital in Bowen Road, and died on a Japanese ship, in October 1942. His name is recorded on a war memorial in Hong Kong, which Pat visited some years ago.

In 1942, while I was an apprentice under training in the Engineering Dept. Drawing Office, I was selected to assist a qualified Technical Officer, undertaking ships engine trials. We travelled via Stranraer in Scotland, to Belfast, and stayed in a hotel called the Eglinton and Winton (now defunct) The ship on which we were carrying out the trials, was HMS Espiegle, a minesweeper being built at Harland and Wolf's shipyard. It was during these trials in Belfast Lough, that the ship's C.O. received a signal, stating, that there was a German U Boat in the near vicinity, and because we were unarmed, we scuttled back to port very smartly. My grandchildren have all been regaled at some time, with the story of my being chased by a U Boat . I remember the Technical Officer that I worked with, was named Patrick (an Irishman) and he drank large quantities of draft Guinness, and introduced me to the brew, which was much smoother than the bottled version available in England. To leave the country and to be able to return, we were issued with yet another special Identity Card, a travel Permit Card which I have shown at Fig.11 and Fig.12.

During the latter 2 years of my apprenticeship, I had to balance my Home Guard duties with my Admiralty work. After 2 years in the Home Guard infantry battalion, I transferred to an Anti-Aircraft Battery on Southsea Common, on the coast. Here I was promoted to Sergeant, and then to 2nd.Lieutenant, and became a

Troop Officer on a Battery mounting 64 rocket guns, and being responsible for the firing of 16 of them. These guns which were operated entirely by Home Guards, were very unsophisticated, and fired 2 rockets off metal rails, after the rounds(about 4 feet long) had been fused with key rings, and the guns aligned for angle and directions, on instructions from the Command Post. As the rockets were all fired together on command, they produced a huge concentrated area of exploding shell in the sky. Army gunners also operated on the site, with 3.7" and 4.5" AA guns. The Home Guard did shoot down at least one Dornier bomber, but our task was primarily to keep the bombers away from the Dock-yard area. During the day I worked on ships in the Dockyard, and this work could encompass almost any engineering work, on steam engines, turbines, diesels, pumps, generators, and ship fittings, like torpedo tubes and gun mountings ie any work that had to be done on the ship in situ. I have successfully slept in a torpedo tube. Ship's engine trials and minesweeping trials, were also part of the job. On one occasion, I recall almost all of the ship's crew, and the dockyard staff on board, were violently sick during minesweeping trials in the Solent, largely due to a heavy swell, and to a very greasy stew that the cook prepared for lunch.

Following an announcement by Ernest Bevin, the then Minis-ter of Labour, in December 1943, some boys of 18 were con-scripted to work in the coal mines, instead of the armed forces. The method of conscription was totally random, every tenth con-script being sent to the mines, and I believe there was no appeal. The 'Bevin Boys' toiled hard to keep up with Britain's insatiable need of energy from coal, to drive the manufacturing machinery, and heat homes. (there was no central heating in those days)

In 1943 we moved to a larger house in The Circle at Southsea, which had a room on the second floor covering the whole of the top of the house. At this time, the Mulberry Harbours were being constructed at Portsmouth Dockyard, for use during the invasion of France, soon to come, and construction workers were being recruited from all over the country. Because of the unused space in our house, we were forced to billet three of these workers in the house, until the construction work was finished. Although inconvenient, mum made them as welcome as possible in those days, and when they left, they thanked her for the kindness she had shown them, but this was typical of mum. On 6th. June 1944 we invaded Europe, landing on the beaches in Northern France.

After I had completed my apprenticeship in October 1943, I was appointed in January 1944, as a Draughtsman / Technical Officer, and was employed at the After Action Repair Depot at Swanmore, an Admiralty Depot, evacuated from Portsmouth Dockyard, to a site some miles north of the dockyard in Hampshire, where we supplied engine spares and boat's equipment, to ships and small craft damaged in action. This job was made more difficult, because the boats / ships crews, were often unable to specify exactly what they wanted, and because engine marques / types, and sizes of underwater fittings, were regularly updated by the manufacturers. A great deal of time was spent referring to manuals, and parts lists, and contacting boat builders and engine makers.

When I joined the Depot our means of transport from the Portsmouth area, was by a 3 ton RN seated lorry, men and women travelling together, and this was where I first met Muriel Hayden. Later in the year we were allocated two buses (one for the office staff and one for the store (one must observe the social distinctions!!) and the drivers took some delight in a bit of racing, with tooting of horns and jeering passengers, to see who could get home first. Muriel will have quite a lot to say about transport, as she was at Swanmore for longer than me. One of the things I remember about the period between March and early June, was the soldiers, tanks and equipment parked alongside the country roads, leading to Swanmore, in the build up to the invasion of France. The soldiers generally cheered us as we went by, but I did wonder later how many of those soldiers survived, and came home at the end of the war. During this period we worked long hours, day and night, as the depot was operational 24 hours a day, and we were allocated the princely night time rations of one tin of baked beans, or a piece of cheese! It was during the night shifts here, that we experienced German V1 rockets, and I counted 20 on one night alone, flying over us, and landing harmlessly in the open countryside. On large cities like London however, they produced much indiscriminate damage.

Spies led by MI6, discovered in 1943, that V2 rockets were being built by Germany. A committee set up in the Ministry of Home Security, expressed extreme concern over the effects of such rockets. Flawed intelligence (where have we heard of that before) brought the government to the verge of panic, and they proposed the move of key Ministries underground, and even considered the total evacuation of London, but the War Cabinet considered that this would be tantamount to acceptance of defeat, and stood firm against this idea. In the event, the reality of the V2 while bad enough, was not as damaging as Churchill's committee had predicted (ie one missile per hour would produce 3600 dead and 100,000 Londoners homeless per day) The V2 a 46ft. conventional supersonic rocket, launched from fixed sites deep inside Germany, carried a 1 ton rather than a 10 ton warhead, and only 1115 were fired at England. The first one fell in Chiswick, London in September 1944, and the last one in March 1945, at Orpington in Kent. They killed 2750 people across southern England, rather than the 167,250 predicted. I do not recall any rockets landing in the Portsmouth area,—they were probably targeted mainly on

London and the suburbs. The introduction of these rockets, was generally considered to be too late to influence the outcome of the war. It is interesting that von Braun the German scientist behind their introduction, was after the war, removed to the USA, to apply his expertise and knowledge, to the introduction of rockets for the American space programme. By late 1944 however, Allied troops were advancing into Germany, and British and American troops crossed the Rhine on 7th. March 1945.

On 22nd. November 1944, after being in force for 5 years, the blackout ended, with the switching on of street lights in various squares and thoroughfares in London, followed by similar action throughout the country, when street lighting was repaired, and became operational again. Blackout curtains, painted windows, hooded car lights etc, became a thing of the past. In December 1944 Britain's home front war effort, was being aided, by the efforts of carefully selected prisoners of war, mostly Italians, who were paid up to six shillings a week to dig potatoes, harvest sugar beet, and generally help on farms. Mostly they were glad to be usefully employed, and were well treated by the locals, some being invited into their homes. A few of these prisoners remained in Britain, and married locally.

By December 1944 the threat of invasion was long past, and the Home Guard was stood down. On 3rd. December 1944, a Home Guard farewell parade took place before the King and Queen, and the royal Princesses Elizabeth and Margaret in Hyde Park. A crowd estimated at around one million, turned out to see 7000 men, drawn from every Command in the country, march through the heart of London. In the evening of the parade, a concert with a cast including Tommy Trinder, Vera Lynn and Cicely Courtnedge, was held in the Albert Hall for the marchers. My local farewell parade was held in the Guildhall Square in Portsmouth, and as an officer (Fig.13) I was invited with my family on to the viewing platform on the Guildhall steps. I still have the invitation card, and my original Home Guard armband. Meanwhile in Germany, Hitler's own Home Guard, the Volkssturm, was being hastily recruited as a last ditch defence against the allied armies, massing at the borders of the Reich.

On 30th April 1945 Hitler committed suicide, and 2 days later Berlin surrendered to the Russian army. On 7th May, Germany surrendered unconditionally, and 8th. May was declared VE (Victory in Europe) day. Winston Churchill announcing the Allied victory said "This is your victory! It is the victory of the cause of freedom in every land. Everyone, man or woman has done their best. In all our long history, we have never seen a greater day than this" Celebrations took place all over the country, with singing and dancing in the streets, with street parties, and church bells ringing for the first time since the war started. In August, the Americans dropped the first ever Atomic Bomb on Hiroshima Japan, and then a second on Nagasaki. Although the Japanese did not officially surrender until the 2nd September of that year, the allies celebrated VJ (Victory in Japan) Day on 15th August, the signing having taken place on board USS Missouri, in Tokyo Bay, to an 11 man delegation led by General MacArthur. On 3rd. September British troops landed back in Hong Kong and Malaysia.

On 5th July 1945 Britain held a General Election, but the result was delayed, to allow the collection of votes of servicemen and women overseas. On 26th July the result, when declared, produced a landslide victory for Labour, over Churchill and the Tories. Voters had cheered Churchill wherever he went during the war, but did not see him as a suitable peace time leader. Such is fame!

During the war years, John Hewinson came home on leave regularly from the army, and I always made a point of being available to see him, and devote as much time as possible with him, to pursue our common interests. "Harry" which is what I was always called by all the Hewinson family, were always pleased to see me, and we were all destined to get together again after the war.

It was while working at Swanmore in 1944, that I met a typist named Múriel on an old RN lorry We got engaged early in 1945, and we were to share the rest of our lives together.

CHAPTER 8

The early post war years

E arly in 1945 I was posted to the Engineer in Chief's Department of the Admiralty at Bath, as a Draughtsman/Technical officer. My duties reflected those at Swanmore, but here at H.Q, we were concerned with the introduction and administration, of spares and equipment depots, known as Spare Parts Distribution Centres (SPDC's). These were being set up at home and abroad, to try to centralise, and improve provision of equipment after the war. (during the war paper work and accounting was often bypassed, when immediate supply to a ship was paramount.). I lodged at a house where there were already 4 other lodgers, but as an Admiralty employee, I was given a bedroom to myself. After 2 weeks I came home on leave, and was surprised to find on my return, I had another Admiralty lodger sharing my bedroom. The other lodger was an ex naval type named Ted Rowe, and we became very friendly, although Ted was much older than me, being a naval pensioner.

In 1945 the war came to an end, and we celebrated VE Day on May 8th. I and my ex Portsmouth colleagues Harry Weatherley, Frank Jenkins, and Phil Chapman, who had been posted to Bath before me, and who lived in the same digs, heard the news on the wireless in the evening, and without permission, we decided to go home for the next few days. We caught a milk train from Bath at midnight, which stopped at almost every station, before arriving at Paddington in the early hours of the morning. At Paddington, we waited on the very crowded platform until about 6-30am, when the first train left for Portsmouth, and by late morning I was knocking on a very surprised Muriel's door. Muriel and I had got engaged earlier in the year, before I was posted to Bath. It is difficult to remember exactly how we spent the next few days, but there was dancing in the streets, street parties, and the ringing of church bells, which had not sounded since the war started, as they were to be used only in the event of an invasion. Our local pub, The Phoenix close to where Muriel lived, did a roaring trade, to which Muriel and I contributed our share. The merrymaking on VJ Day, later in the year, seemed less outgoing, mainly I think because fewer people in England, had had direct contact with the fighting in the Far East. It did mean the release of prisoners from Hong Kong and Singapore however.

As Muriel and I were now engaged, I spent as many weekends as possible in Portsmouth. My friend Harry Weatherley purchased a war surplus motor cycle, and when our home weekends coincided, I would ride pillion passenger to get home. This was much quicker and cheaper than the train, which took about 4 hours from Bath, and required you to change trains at Salisbury although we did operate a 'fiddle' which allowed us to drastically reduce the cost. When I stayed in Bath, many weekends were spent rowing on the River Avon with my Portsmouth colleagues. We hired the boat at Bath, and rowed up the river to the lock at Bradford on Avon, carrying the boat past the riverside pub at Bathampton. These trips were characterised by continual singing, as we rowed. All of us had reasonable voices, and we specialised in singing song from the shows and films. I learned many new songs by heart on these outings, because Frank Jenkins seemed to know them all, and started us off. Many other weekends when this was not possible (Frank and Phil got married in 1946) were spent walking in the Somerset countryside, mainly with Ted Rowe. On one occasion when Ted had gone home for the weekend, I and another of our lodgers, went on a walk, and finished up at a pub in Radstock. Not realising the potency of raw cider (or perhaps thinking we could take it) we both had two pints, and then waited outside for the 2 o'clock bus back to Bath. We woke up on the grass verge, to hear the driver of the 4 o'clock bus hooting at us, and saying that this was the last bus back to Bath for some hours.

Our landlady in the digs was a Welsh harpie named Credwyn Gifford, whose evening meals consisted of mashed potatoes, boiled cabbage, and gravy, with the very occasional piece of meat. Fortunately I could buy a very reasonable lunch in the Admiralty canteen, so I didn't starve. But Ted and I devised a scheme, to get some slices of brown dripping for supper, after Mr. and Mrs. Gifford had gone to bed. We scraped all the brown from the bottom of the dish for our bread. We then placed the dish (fortunately a metal one) on a low gas, so that the dripping melted. We then left it to cool, so that by morning there was a nice flat surface on the top of the dripping, and no one was the wiser. During my 2 years in Bath, Harry Weatherley and I joined the Admiralty Male voice choir. Our repertoire was not extensive, and our concerts few, but I enjoyed it as it was the first organised singing I had done since the war started.

The first years after the war were a period of preparing for the future. Dorothy got married to Russell, whom she had met through me, as he was a fellow officer in the Home Guard, and Mum moved three times to different houses in Southsea, finishing up in a house owned by Russell. Pat, Shirley, and Michael, returned from Australia late in 1945, and at Xmas, Muriel and I made some home made Crackers for the children's first Xmas in

England, as these were unobtainable in the shops. Pat, and Reg,, who was also now living in Portsmouth, working with Rusell, had at first decided to emigrate to Australia, where Pat had spent the war years, but after Reg decided to marry Maisie, this fell through.

I was not happy to remain as a Draughtsman / Technical officer, as the pay and conditions were not as good as in some other grades of the Civil Service. I set my sights on the Executive grade, but in the meantime until the post war exams were finalised, I had to settle for the Clerical Officer's exam, which was the first of the post war reconstruction exams. I passed easily, but to my disgust, I was appointed to the Customs and Excise Department at Southampton. I was not happy with the narrow and bureaucratic attitudes in the Custom House, and I think they were as pleased as I was, when I was transferred to a Customs station in Southampton Docks. Here I was working with Customs Officers on a station, where barrels of wine imported from South Africa, were Bonded, and tested by sampling, so we always managed to have a glass of wine (of unused samples of course) at lunch time. It was at this time Muriel and I decided to get married, and not surprisingly, my wedding present from the Officers was a set of wine glasses..

Muriel and I got married on 23rd. September 1947, at St Mark's Church Portsmouth, and we held our reception at the nearby Angerstein Hall. Greta, Muriel's sister, and Shirley, my niece, were bridesmaids, and my brother Reg. was best man. Photographers in those days did not attend weddings, so we all visited the photographer's studio for the wedding photos. (Figs.14 & 15) A friend of ours had managed to get hold of a roll of wartime RAF film (date unknown), and took as many pictures as he could. The results were poor, but we were thankful for anything we could get, in those days of rationing and shortages. Clothes as well as food were rationed. I had saved up enough clothing coupons to purchase a new suit for the wedding, and chose a dark chalk stripe. To my horror when it arrived, it turned out to be solid black. I felt I was going to a funeral rather than a wedding, and I don't think I ever wore it again, but like so many things in those days, we had to accept what we could get.

We were luckier with the honeymoon arrangements. As I worked for the Customs and Excise in Southampton Docks, which were run by the Southern Railway, I was entitled to a concession fare anywhere on their services, and I got a reduced fare passage to Jersey, on one of their cross channel ferries. Muriel's stepfather (Bert), was a steward on one of these ferries, and he managed to secure a cabin for us on his ship, which was an improvement on the upper deck accommodation I had managed to book. We spent our honeymoon at Swanson's Hotel, situated on the seafront at Jersey, about which I can remember very little, but when we went back to Jersey some years later, it was still there. Jersey was getting back to normal after the occupation, and some things were better there, than in England. For a wedding present, Bert managed to get us a decorated china tea set, something unobtainable in England, where you could only buy plain white china.

Our first home after we were married, was one bedroom, in Muriel's mothers house, but after a while we were offered rooms in a nearby house. This offer unfortunately fell through, but later we managed to get furnished rooms (Lounge/dining room, a bedroom and shared bathroom kitchen and toilet facilities) The other occupant of the house was Elsie Bridges, who with her brother, owned the house. We were vetted very carefully!! Elsie worked at Lloyds Bank at North End, and she was later joined by her new husband Cyril, who also worked at the bank. We liked Elsie very much, but Cyril got on our nerves, especially when he came downstairs in the morning singing. We also thought he was a bit of a drip. We lived like this from 1947 to 1951, (Fig.16) when we eventually moved to Plymouth. .

In 1948, I had joined a Freemasons Lodge in Portsmouth. Although I knew nothing of their activities, I was encouraged to join by my Grandfather.(Mum's Dad) who had been the Master of a Lodge, and he recommended me. I was in good company, because Reg. Flewin the captain of Portsmouth football team, joined just before me. I was a regular attendee at the Lodge, but it wasn't long before I moved to Plymouth, and after that I only visited other Lodges by invitation. The only time I joined another Lodge, was in Johore Bahru Malaya some years later (See page 82) In 1948 we also went on holiday to Butlins holiday camp. Holiday opportunities were scarce at this time, and while we enjoyed it, it wasn't us, and we never ventured there again.

I had taken another Civil Service exam for Clerical Officer in 1948, which enabled me to move back to Portsmouth, from Southampton, at a better salary, and I was appointed to the Superintending Naval Store Officers (SNSO) Department, at Portsmouth dockyard. I had been friends with Frank Pascoe, since our apprentice days, and Muriel, Frank and I, worked together at Swanmore. We exchanged evening visits with Frank and his wife Joyce, and we decided to go on a holiday together, to St.Anton in Austria in 1950. Frank by now worked in London as a Customs Officer, and he made all the arrangements. Muriel and I took the train to London, staying overnight. Next day we all took the train to Folkestone, and crossed to Calais, where we boarded the coach, and started our journey, stopping overnight at Challons sur Marne. Next day we continued, making comfort stops at Domremy (Joan of Arc's birthplace) and Basle. The last stage to St Anton was very scary.

The coach company had underestimated the time required, and it was a very dark and perilous journey, over the mountains. The driver had to stop twice to freshen himself up, but we eventually arrived late at night, tired and happy to get there.

While we were there we made trips to Landek, and Innsbruck in Austria, St Moritz in Switzerland, and Castobello in Italy. We also visited all the snow covered passes, (the Flexen and Arlberg in Austria, and the Julier in Switzerland), and went to the top of the Galzig which was 6500 ft. A place of particular interest was Hochfinstermunz, which is situated at the point where the borders of Austria, Switzerland, and Italy meet, and from where you can see all three countries. We also witnessed a local wedding, and on the Whit Monday, saw a festival in full Tyrolean costume at Pettneu, a local village. After an excellent holiday, we returned via Strasbourg, Rheims, (where we were attracted by the beautiful singing in the cathedral), and Calais, where we boarded the ferry, for the final part of our journey.

Fig.1 The Harrison family circa 1910. Gordon's paternal grandmother is seated with his father at the top right.

Fig.2 Gordon's maternal grandfather circa 1910 in RAMC uniform

Fig.3 Gordon's mother and father photographed during the 1914-1918 war.

Fig.4 Muriel's mother at our wedding in 1947.

Fig.5 Muriel's Paternal grandparents.

Fig.6 Muriel's maternal grandparents

Fig.7 Gordon –Head Choirboy at Hilsea Garrison Church 1940

Fig.8 Gordon's Wartime Identity Card (External)

GORDON & MURIEL HARRISON

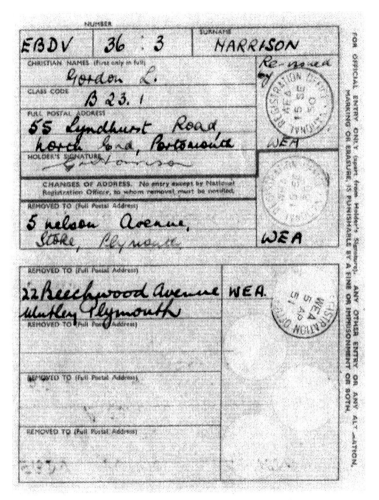

Fig.9 Gordon's Wartime Identity card (inside)

Fig.10 Gordon in Home Guard uniform 1941

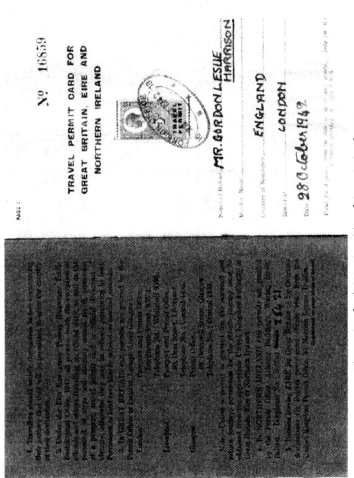

Fig.11 Gordon's Wartime Travel Permit Card 1942

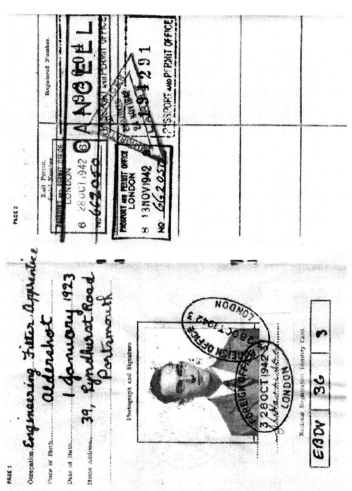

Fig.12 Gordon's Wartime Travel Permit Card 1942 (Inside)

Fig.13 Gordon in Home Guard uniform in 1944.

Fig.14 Muriel and Gordon on their wedding day 23rd. September 1947.

Fig.15 Muriel on our wedding day 23rd.September 1947.

Fig.16 Muriel and Gordon circa 1946

Fig.17 Norman, Doris and Roger with us on a picnic in Cornwall 1951

Fig.18 Neil 18 months old with the Harrison family

Fig.19 Gordon's office staff Singapore 1954

Fig.20 Parties given by contractors in Singapore to UK staff.
—C.K.Soh (top) and Tay Koh Yat (bottom)

Fig.21 We sailed in the Corfu to Singapore in 1954

Fig.22 Muriel and other choristers in Singapore Church 1956

Fig.23 Homeward bound on M.V.Oranje 1957

A children's organised party aboard the Oranje

Fig.24 Gala night dinner aboard the Oranje

Fig.25 Wan Tai our Amah and Neil and Rosemary in the garden of the bungalow

Fig.26 Our bungalow at Lewis Rd. and the Mosque opposite

Fig.27 Some of the costumes at our Halloween
fancy dress party in 1963

Fig.28 Gordon's staff photo at Copenacre 1983

Fig.29 Frustrated by the war years academic
success comes at last in 1987

CHAPTER 9

The start of the mobile years

I was at last able to take the Civil Service Executive examination in 1950, which I was successful in passing. At my interview in London, which formed part of the exam., I relaxed in the evening by going to the theatre to see a show called Brigadoon. By the middle of 1950 I was appointed as an Executive Officer at SNSO Devonport. During my spell of duty at Bath, Muriel had not joined me, and remained in her job at the Engineering Department at Portsmouth Dockyard, and she did not join me straight away, when I was posted to Plymouth. I spent many week ends, travelling back and forth to Portsmouth, either by train, or by coach, until I was able to find suitable accommodation for us. During this period of separation, I found some digs at the home of Mrs. Gould (and Henry). Mrs Gould couldn't make a decent cup of tea, or a good fire, but she did make the best pasties I have ever tasted, and she became a lifelong friend. Henry was a dog of character, who hated the postman, but could always tell when Muriel was approaching the front door.

At this time another young Executive Officer was appointed to the Department, and as we were the same age, we became good friends, and remain so to this day. Norman Smith had married Doris in 1945, and he managed to find temporary digs for them in Devonport, and then rented a house in Saltash, just across the water in Cornwall. When Muriel joined me early in 1952, the four of us were to make regular visits to each others homes, and also to make trips into the Cornish countryside.(Fig 17) Norman had managed to buy an old Morris 10, and our trips included a trip to see the "Floral Dance" at Helston.

Muriel and I had managed to obtain an unfurnished flat, in the top half of a house, rebuilt after the war, at 22 Beechwood Avenue in Plymouth. We needed furniture for the first time in our lives, so we went to White's furniture shop in Portsmouth, and bought the minimum essentials, a bed, two easy chairs, a dining table, four dining chairs, a sideboard, and some carpet. This was additional to the Alba radiogram, which was our first purchase after our wedding in 1947. Our furniture was the first made after the wartime 'Utility' furniture, and it speaks volumes for its quality, that we still use the sideboard, and the dining table, and chairs, and the radiogram was only disposed of when we moved to Box.

Our flat was owned by a lady named Sylvia, who occupied the ground floor flat, with her husband. She was always complaining about something, and had a habit of locking the front door, before she retired to bed, at about 9-30. The most memorable example of this was in June 1953. Muriel and I had gone to a fireworks display in Home Park, and did not return to the house until about 11 o'clock, only to find the front door locked. We rang the bell, and knocked on the door, for nearly half an hour, before we could make anyone hear us, and when the door was finally opened, all the landlady could say was 'I thought you were in'. Nevertheless we got our own back, because about 1 o'clock that morning, Muriel who was pregnant, started her contractions, and we rushed her to Freedom Fields Hospital, and by 10-30 that night, Neil was born, a healthy 8lbs 4oz. Unfortunately, Muriel suffered from septic stitches after the birth, and had to go back into hospital. Neil was so young, and I could not look after him at home, and because he could not be accommodated in the hospital with Muriel, he was sent to a nursing home to be looked after. I could not bring myself to visit, and then have to leave him again, but he was well looked after there, and after a short while, Muriel and I went to the nursing home, and brought him home. The staff said what a good baby he had been while he was with them, and he remained a happy baby with us, always waking in the morning with a smile on his face. Gladys, Muriel's mother, then came to stay, to help mother and baby settle in.

We wanted Neil to be christened at St. Mark's church where we had been married, and while we had no problems when we were married, the new vicar was reluctant to let us use the church for the christening, because Muriel had not been confirmed. After some prevarication however, he did eventually agree, but not before making Muriel feel very embarrassed. Neil got his own back however, by wetting the vicar, and crying during the ceremony. Neil's Godparents were my brother Reg. and Greta, Muriel's sister.(Muriel was later confirmed in the church at the Naval Base in Singapore, by the Bishop of Singapore)

During this spell of duty at Plymouth, I was responsible for the management of Royal Fleet Auxiliary (RFA) tankers, and supply ships, within the Port, and for the receipt, issue, and stock-holding of fuel. I managed to get a trip on a RFA oil tanker, through the French canals, to where we were to deliver fuel oil to a French installation. The trip was from Friday afternoon to Monday afternoon, so I had to get leave from my boss, and enjoyed the free boat trip. As part of my duties I was also required to make annual trips to Pembroke Dock, in South Wales. Here we had a fuel depot, for which I was managerially responsible, and I had to undertake checks on the specification, and quantity, of the fuel in the tanks. This required me to climb to the top of the fuel tanks, with a storehouseman, who made dips to ascertain the level of the oil, and to obtain samples. These inspections were usually made at the end of summer, when the fuel was warmer and more fluid, but the top of a 100 ft. high tank, in an exposed tank farm, can be pretty breezy and uncomfortable.

While my duties in connection with fuelling ships usually meant oil fuel, the Navy still ran a fewer older Fisheries Protection vessels, which burned coal. At one period, when they were having difficulty obtaining stocks ashore (to prevent these ships having to return to the UK), I went to the Scilly Isles to negotiate with a supplier. He was proving difficult, because he objected to the red tape associated with the payment documentation. After some discussion with him, I managed to get him to agree a method which was simpler for him, but at the same time safeguarded the Naval accounting. My superiors at Headquarters were suitably impressed

As head of the Fuel Section, I was responsible for allocating the fuel oil deliveries, in visiting fuel tankers, to the shore fuel tanks. The storage tanks at Devonport, were situated on both banks of the river Hamoaze, which separates Devon from Cornwall, the main depot being on the Cornwall side, at Torpoint. My staff maintained records of the capacity of the dozens of fuel tanks, and the type of fuel they contained, and these details were updated weekly, so that when a tanker was due I knew, which tank(s) could be utilised. The tanker was met in Plymouth Sound, by the tugs of the Captain of the Dockyard's Dept., and taken up the Hamoaze, to the appropriate fuel depot. Only once did an error occur due to faulty records, and I had to get my Superintending Officer, to phone the Captain of the Dockyard, while the tanker was under tow, to radio and amend the tug's destination, and arrange alternative berthing arrangements. There were one or two red faces that day, and a few "don't let it happen again "comments, and it didn't.

A very interesting part of my job while I was at Plymouth, involved the construction of a new jetty, with its associated pipelines, and the updating of the boiler house equipment at Torpoint. As the head of the Fuel Section, I was a member of the Dockyard team, which included mechanical and structural engineers, planning and progressing the work. Because of my background as an engineer apprentice, and technical officer, my comments were readily accepted in the committee, and I was able to make a reasonable, and relevant input, over the months of the jetty building, and the boiler house refit. The work did present some difficulties during this period, as it was necessary to keep the oil fuel depot fully operational at all times, but the work proceeded extremely smoothly, and there were no major problems to my recollection.

CHAPTER 10

Singapore 1954-1957

In 1954 I was appointed to Singapore, for duty ashore or afloat, and so that our families could see more of Neil, after we went home to Portsmouth for Xmas, (see Fig 18) Muriel stayed in Portsmouth with her mother. During these two months, I stayed with Mrs.Gould again, as our furniture at No.22 Beechwood Avenue, Plymouth had to be put in store, because it was not needed at Singapore, where our accommodation was already furnished. I made a number of weekend trips between Plymouth and Portsmouth, on a coach provided for service personnel, and I remember these trips being some of the coldest I have ever made. The unheated coach left Portsmouth at about midnight By the time I arrived in Devonport, I was totally shrammed, and because the coach arrived at about 5-30 am., I had to walk around a local park, until about 7-00 am, when I knew Mrs.Gould would be getting up. On March 7th.1954, Muriel and I caught the train at Cosham station, to Southampton, and boarded the P&O SS Corfu.(see Fig.21) A number of people unacquainted with the situation in Singapore, thought that we were taking a young child into the jungle.

The voyage to Singapore was a welcome experience. We travelled via Port Said, the Suez Canal, Aden and Bombay. In England in 1954, many foodstuffs were still rationed, but on the Corfu was available in quantities and variety, we had not seen since before the war. We took full advantage of what was on offer, and for three weeks lived life to the full (after we had passed through the Bay of Biscay) We travelled out with a departmental colleague and his family, Harry Smerdon, his wife Steve(Ruth), and children Pauline and Peter. We soon met on board, and became firm friends. Suitable summer clothes were difficult to obtain at home in March, and it was no surprise therefore to find that Muriel, and Steve, had bought a dress of identical pattern, from Marks and Spencer. Fortunately the colours were different. Surprisingly I also met on board, an old friend Ron. Merritt, who had been on the Home Guard gun site with me, during the war, and whom I had not seen since 1945. He also had his wife Joyce and three children Jane, Ann, and Stephen with him, and the three families were to see a lot of each other in Singapore.

On arrival in Singapore Muriel and I, and Steve and Harry, moved into Rochdale Guest House. It was a slightly rundown colonial style house, owned by a Eurasian woman, who had lived in Singapore during the occupation by the Japanese. While Muriel and Steve spent the days exploring the town, and shopping, Harry and I travelled up the Thompson road to the Naval Base, which was at the northern tip of the island. Harry had brought a new Ford Consul out from England, and once the formalities were completed, we used his car to drive to and from work. Taxis were plentiful and cheap, so the girls used these. I had to take my share of the driving however, and so I started driving lessons with a Chinese instructor named Michael Lim, in an old Morris Minor, and fortunately passed the test first time.

Driving in Singapore was hazardous! There were large monsoon drains on both sides of the road, driving standards by the Mercedes taxi drivers were abysmal, and in Chinatown, where we had to drive for experience, it was quite normal to see bicycle riders and pedestrians, loaded down with water cans on a pole across their shoulders, live chickens in a basket, and hawkers so loaded down with their wares, that you could hardly see them. The driving test started at the Police HQ in the centre of town, and after completing the road test, you were required to perform vertical and parallel parking, between four poles, set up outside the building. There was a deep monsoon drain alongside these poles, and there was always a large collection of Indian and Chinese boys, cheering your efforts, and hoping you would drive into the drain. If you did, you obviously failed the test, and these boys then offered their assistance (paid of course), to lift your car out of the drain. Muriel still had this pleasure to come on a future trip. Having passed my test, I invested in a used Morris Oxford, which lasted me for a number of years, both at Singapore and at home.

As soon as we arrived in Singapore, we were invited by the Commander in Chief Far East Fleet (Admiral Sir Charles Lamb), to a "small dance" at Phoenix Park, his residence. We were in quite exalted company, but after we had made our salutations to the C in C, and had a couple of drinks, and a dance to the Royal Marines band, we left. Our uniform in Singapore was the same for all Naval staff—white shirts, white shorts, and long white stockings. Service officers wore caps outside the office, but although civilians were not required to wear hats, we were expected to salute the quarter deck, when visiting ships in the Dockyard. On arrival, most of us bought 'Pussers' issue, but as the shorts tended to be quite long, we resorted to 'Toothy Wong' for our replacements, as these could be made to order, and were slightly more fashionable. Toothy (no prizes for guessing why he acquired this appellation), had a shop just outside the Naval Base Sembawang gate, and could run you up a set of shirts and shorts, in just a few days. His was a very popular establishment, and all the children who entered the shop, could expect a free 'Green Spot', a well known orange drink. Shoes were another item which could be made to measure in a few days, but the quality of the leather was not as good as in the UK, so did not last as long. Toothy could also make you a lightweight tropical suit, and I still have mine.

After a short time in the Guest House, the Smerdon and Harrison families, moved into a modern 3 bedroom bungalow, on an estate called Braddell Heights. We employed a cook boy, an Amah (his wife) and a Khebun (gardener), and Harry and I shared the costs, which was very beneficial for both our families. The cook boy and his wife were Chinese, but the Khebun was a Malay. Now I was sharing the driving to the Naval Base with Harry, Steve could use her car for trips to town. While living at Braddell Heights I killed my first (and only) snake. The cookboy rushed in one day shouting 'very bad, very bad.' Neil was playing on the front patio of the bungalow, not far from the snake, so I rushed out with something heavy, and hit it on the head until it was dead. It turned out to be a small black cobra, which because it was dangerous, had to be reported. The police investigated, and found a nest of the snakes in an adjacent garden, and thankfully killed them all. While living at Braddell Heights I also learned what night soil was, because it was used extensively on the fields of crops, and vegetables, on the local farms. This was one of the reasons we always bought our produce from the larger shops in Singapore town, which imported fruit, vegetables, eggs etc from Australia. Milk was local, but came from specially maintained farm animals.

Saturday afternoons were usually set aside for family shopping, (we worked in the morning), and Sundays were often spent all day, at the Singapore Swimming Club. Here my curry lunches were something to behold, and were washed down with copious quantities of Tiger or Anchor beer. This is where Muriel and I began our lifelong love, of Malay curries, which used numerous side dishes of fruit, egg, coconut etc. We also frequented the Johore Bahru guest house, for tea on Saturday and Sunday afternoons, and visited the RAF Changi Officers Club, on the East side of the Island, where they had safe sea bathing, in what was known as a Pagar, a fenced off area.

Accommodation in the Naval Base was limited. You went on to a waiting list as soon as you arrived on the Station, and it was about 18 months before we all moved into the Base. Most of the bungalows were the old colonial type, and you had the choice of one of these, or a modern furnished flat. Both of our families chose the flats. Although many hotels and shops were air conditioned at this time, the flats relied on large airy windows, and overhead fans, but they were very well furnished, and appointed. In the flat, we employed (secondly), a cook/amah called Mabel, who unusually was a Chinese Christian. Mabel was a reasonable cook with a limited range. She and Neil got on well together, and being an older woman, she was not demanding of time off. Our first amah, Tan, had been dismissed for having a man in her room, for which her father strongly disapproved .

The traders in Singapore, and in the Naval Base, were helpful, and anxious to obtain and hold your custom. So much so that at Xmas, instead of them expecting Xmas boxes, they gave you gifts. We obtained quite a bit of our Noritake china in this way. Entertainment in the Base was limited to a cinema, which ran weekly films, but there were always private dinner parties, and cocktail parties on the ships, and we were frequently invited to parties, (usually Chinese food with plenty of drinks), by contractors, who operated within the Base (Fig.20). We were invited to a fancy dress party, at a friend's house, which while very good, was completely diminished by our fancy dress party, during our next tour. There were also a number of good air conditioned cinemas in Singapore, and many colourful local events to see, especially at Chinese New Year, when dragon and lion dances were performed at various outdoor areas. There were also the Wayangs. These were outdoor Chinese theatres, which told their stories in acting and song. They were very colourful in background scenery and costume, and the actors were usually covered in face paint, with a predominantly white background. We didn't understand any of it of course, but it was interesting to watch, and very noisy. Equally colourful, but gruesome, was the Tiger Balm Gardens, with its grotesque statuettes. There was only one elephant on Singapore Island, so we took Neil to see him. For a small fee, his owner persuaded him to work, pulling a few logs around.

There were no tigers on the island, although the northern part of the Naval Base was called Rimau, the Chinese name for tiger, so there must have been some there at one time. The wild life was generally limited to small lizards, and insects like the praying mantis. Mosquitos were plentiful, but their treatment by the authorities, especially in the monsoon drains, was rigorous, and Malaria and Yellow Fever were almost unknown. Mosquito nets round beds were however prevalent all over the island, for Europeans. The numerous Geckos, (small lizards) usually referred to as chick chacks, which ran up and down the walls, were a novelty, but completely harmless. In 1956 Muriel joined the Naval Base church choir, and there is a picture of her with other members of the choir, which was composed of ladies and boys, at Fig.22. Like me she enjoyed singing, and took advantage of this opportunity.

Norman and Doris arrived on station about half way through our tour, and the families spent a lot of time together, especially at Xmas, and on our island trips. For these latter, a group of us hired a launch and crew from the dockyard, and visited local islands, the most popular being known as Coney Island. These picnics, on sandy beaches, with clean water for swimming, were very popular. The Commodore of the Naval Base was a friendly and approachable officer, and Neil soon became quite a favourite, possibly because of his fair curly hair. If the Commodore saw Neil out walking with Muriel in the Base, he would stop, and invite him to drive into the dockyard in his service car. Neil was suitably impressed with driving in a car, with a Commodore's flag on the front, and Mr.Singh the turbaned Indian driver. In 1955, I dressed up as father Xmas at our departmental party for children, where I handed out presents. When it came to Neil's turn he didn't recognise me!!

In the office my staff were a mix of Malays, Indians, and Chinese (See Fig.19) While I was responsible for Naval Base transport, I had to interview drivers who had had accidents, and my interpreter was a Malay clerk, who worked in my office, named Salleh bin Younos. I can't remember exactly how it started, but Salleh (now a Mohd. having visited Mecca) and I started to exchange Xmas cards. I also sent him RN journals, and he sent me first day covers, with Malaya stamp issues. We still exchange Xmas cards, and he still sends me FDC's throughout the year. Some years ago I tried to stop Salleh from sending these covers, which can be quite expensive, and are issued regularly to generate finance, and because I had to stop sending in return the Journals, which had ceased to be published. He was most upset, and sent me a letter saying, you didn't count the cost when it came to old friendships. How's that for loyalty? When we left Singapore, my staff collected, and bought us presents of a clock, a large Chinese ginger jar, a Balinese statuette (both of which we still have) and a toy for Neil—most generous, considering how little they earned in comparison to us.

The local bus service, which also provided contract buses, to bring dockyard workers to the Naval Base from Singapore, was run by a firm called Tay Koh Yat. Old Mr Tay had an MBE, and was very proud of it, and occasionally invited staff from the Base to dinner at his home, to admire his MBE, prominently displayed on the wall (Fig 20 bottom) When Mr. Tay died we went to his funeral. This was a traditional Chinese affair, with numerous lorries decorated with flowers, and paper models of his furniture and effects, which were later burnt, so they would be available to him in the next world. There were also a number of Chinese bands on lorries, (more noise than music), which accompanied the funeral procession. One of these bands went in the opposite direction to the funeral lorries, to lure away any evil spirits from the actual burial. It was undoubtedly the most colourful and noisiest funeral we had ever seen, or were likely to see again.

During this tour of duty because of the emergency, with the communists operating all over Malaya, travel by road outside of Johore Bahru was prohibited, without a special police convoy, and because of this, we did not have holidays up country at Fraser's Hill, or elsewhere. At the end of our tour of duty, we could choose between sailing all the way home, or sailing to Italy on an Italian line ship, and driving the rest of the way home through Europe. Harry and Steve chose the latter way, and we waved them off from the dockside, but Muriel and I chose the pleasurable way, and were lucky to get berths on the ORANJE, a Dutch liner a picture of which is shown at Fig.23. Once again we had a marvellous voyage, calling at Capetown, and Las Palmas on the way. A trip ashore in Capetown entailed climbing the hills around the

Table Mountain, and searching for wild flowers, which abounded there. The voyage was slightly spoiled for Neil, because the younger children had to attend the nursery, for a large part of the day, which Neil was not happy about, but apparently this was the rule on all Dutch ships. A picture of a children's party and the gala night dinner on board is at fig.24.

CHAPTER 11

England 1957-1961

We landed at Southampton, on a cold frosty morning in April, with the temperature in the 30's. After the average temperature of 94 in Singapore, we felt cold. Ken and Greta who had got married in1953, before we left to go to Singapore, and Bert. Greta's Father, came to meet us at the docks. We stayed with Muriel's mother Gladys, in St. Chad's Avenue. She had saved enough coal for a fire, on our first day home, but from then on we had no heating in the house. Gladys didn't seem to understand, that we felt cold, although Bert her husband, who had lived abroad did. I collected the car from the docks in London, after it had been cleared through Customs and cleaned, (the preservation grease etc used for protection during the sea voyage home), but as there was no garage at St. Chad's Avenue, I kept the car at a commercial garage nearby. When I returned to the UK, although I had passed my driving test in Singapore, I had to take it again, to obtain a British licence, but was allowed to use an International licence for 12 months, in the interim. I took my test in the London suburbs, and again passed first time.

We used the car for our weekend trips, house hunting in London, (I had been posted back to the Admiralty) . At first we left Neil at home with Muriel's Mum, but as this was not successful, we subsequently took him with us. Although we had saved money in

Singapore, London house prices were high, and we had to settle for what we could afford. After about 3 months, we eventually found a small 3 bedroom semi detached house, in North Cheam Surrey, and the contracts exchanged. During this period, I travelled up to my London office, at the Admiralty, by train. I caught the 7-27am from Portsmouth each morning, and arrived home in the evening about 7-30pm. By the time I had eaten my evening meal, it was time to go to bed, ready for another early start next morning. At that time we were still working on Saturday mornings, and by the time I got home on Saturday afternoon, there was little left of it. .It was a tiring and frustrating 3 months, and I think we were all glad, when it was over We eventually moved into our new home at 49 St.Margarets Avenue. The house was small, but had a long garden, and a well built brick garage, but the garage was situated at the back of the house, and was accessed by a joint drive, between our house, and our neighbour's. The Morris Oxford now registered as NTP 999, was quite wide, and the drive narrow, and I had many anxious moments and a few scratches to show, while reversing back down the sideway, and curving back into the garage. I subsequently discovered the previous owner had a motorcycle, and sidecar, so he had no difficulty negotiating the drive.

In 1957 Neil was four, and when he was five, he attended Park Farm infants school, at the end of St.Margarets Avenue. There Neil discovered a friend called Gordon, who was of similar age, and lived in the road, and these two became firm friends, during the four years we lived there. The house was reasonably close to the shops on the London road, which included a pub, called the Queen Vic. and to the school, but for me, the journey to work consisted of a 10 minute walk to the London Road, a short bus journey to Worcester Park station, a train journey to Waterloo station, and then either a two stop journey on the underground to

Charing Cross, or a walk over the Charing Cross footbridge. I usually found it quicker to walk. The return journey in the evening, because we were working irregular hours, meant getting home anytime between 6-30 and 7-30. I usually managed to see the children just before they went to bed, after they had helped me eat my dinner.

Sometime after I started this appointment, the Saturday morning duty was cancelled, and a five day week was introduced. Then we had a full weekend as a family. Sometimes we would visit Greta and Ken, who lived at Greenwich, or Steve and Harry, who lived quite close at Stoneleigh, but as we now owned our first TV, we watched that a lot. Neil and I, and sometimes Gordon, watched the Whirlybirds, and Robin Hood on Saturday, and William Tell, and the Last of the Mohicans on Sunday. There was however a very long garden to look after, grass to be cut, and a large vegetable area to be cultivated. Potatoes were a good filler, and we had our own for quite a good part of the year, but I usually planted too many lettuce, which we could not eat in time, and some of them bolted.

Neil and Gordon belonged to a local cinema club, so on most Saturday mornings, they watched films, and purchased fish and chips on the way home. I hope they were better behaved than we were, on our Saturday afternoon visits to the "Empire", or bug hutch as it was popularly known.

My office in the Admiralty building, overlooked Horse Guards Parade, and I was able to take Neil into my office, to watch the Trooping of the Colour. We also visited a circus in London, and walked back over the Charing Cross footbridge at night, and Neil was very impressed to see all the lights on the shipping, on the Thames. I honestly think he thought that more interesting than the circus.

In 1958 Rosemary was born, and once again Muriel had problems. She was born at home, at St. Margaret's Avenue, but after the birth, Muriel started to haemorrhage, and I was despatched to the nearest phone box, to call the hospital for the blood wagon, which had different types of blood on board, and a doctor to administer it. This was a very new scheme, and Muriel was lucky to be able to take advantage of it. She was carried off to hospital in the ambulance, on a drip, and she and Rosemary had to stay in hospital for a while, until she became stronger. Her own doctor, Dr. Rosenour, who was called to the birth, was a real worrier, and scary cat. The nurse who delivered the baby (with my help of course), was a very kind and efficient person however. Neil and I had to make do on our own for a few days, but our neighbours Ted and Vi Payne, were kind enough to look after Neil in the evenings, when I visited Muriel in hospital.

During Rosemary's first year, Neil contracted mumps, and passed it on to Muriel and Rosemary. For some reason, although I have no recollection of having mumps as a child, I did not catch it on this occasion. However while we were in Cheam, we noticed that both Neil and Rosemary had developed a turning eye Both had to wear patches, (Neil on the left eye and Rosemary on the right), to try to strengthen the weaker eye, and both were very good about it. Muriel spent a tremendous amount of time, taking them both to the hospital at Epsom. I was not always able to get time off, to take them in the car, and on these occasions, she had the problem of two children, a push chair, and two bus journeys to contend with. Eventually both children had their operations. Neil was as usual a model patient, and the ward sister was expecting the same from Rosemary.-some hope- Rosemary was her usual ebullient self, refusing to sit in the hospital bath, because it had a water stain in it, and she was according to the sister, generally difficult. As she left the ward to come home, she was busily and loudly telling her ward mates, that she was leaving to go home, and they had to stay in. It wasn't easy for Muriel and I to visit them in hospital, and then leave them behind, and there were a few tears, but it had to be done. Fortunately both operations wee successful at the time, although both had some remedial work done on their eyes, some 40 years later.

In North Cheam, there was a beautiful Park called Nonsuch Park, close by, and we visited it a lot during the summer months. Apart from the flower gardens and walks, there was a large pond, which Neil regularly used for sailing his boats, something which he enjoyed very much. He also had another regular and well loved haunt, when we visited relatives at Portsmouth. I would take him to the ruined Portchester Castle, and he and I would climb the tower, and survey the world from the battlements. Afterwards we would play football or cricket, in the extensive grounds, which surrounded the castle.

Just after Rosemary was born in1958, Russell, Dorothy's second husband died, and she, and Nicky their son, came to stay with us in Cheam, for a few days. Russell had met Dorothy, when he and I were officers together, on the Home Guard battery, at Southsea. Perhaps because Nicky was missing his father, he was quite belligerent, and led Neil into a number of scrapes, while he was with us. Unlike Neil's christening, we had no such problems with Rosemary. At Cheam, our nearest church was St. Oswald's, where Neil attended Sunday school. We arranged for Rosemary's christening there and everything went off smoothly. Rosemary's Godparents were Reg. my brother, and Greta, Muriel's sister.

Although we had many happy times at Cheam, the commuting was boring, and time consuming, and when by chance a vacancy arose at Singapore, which had to be filled quickly, Muriel and I jumped at the opportunity. During my tour of duty in London, I had been promoted to Higher Executive Officer, and was getting the benefit of a good rise in salary. I decided to spend some of this on a new car, to take to Singapore, (you could get a car tax free if you were exporting it), and so I bought a Ford Classic. This was a brand new model, the first with 5 forward gears, and other refinements, and in the event, mine became the first model to arrive in Singapore, and caused quite a stir. I could now dispose of the Morris Oxford, and offered it to my brother Reg. The transfer did not go well, as on the journey from Cheam to Essex, where Reg. lived, Reg's son managed to damage the engine. Because of this Reg said he had to sell the car as scrap, and wouldn't therefore pay me for it. As I had spent quite a lot of time preparing the car for the transfer, and as Ken, Greta's husband had also asked me if he could buy it, I was not amused. We were due to fly to Singapore on this occasion, and when we took our taxi to Stansted airport, to catch our flight at midnight, none of us looked back and regretted leaving the house.

CHAPTER 12

Singapore 1961-1964

We left Stansted airport on a chartered Britannia aircraft. To cut costs, the Admiralty had stopped sea trips abroad, and made civilians, use flights, being used for service personnel. Although we were given the best seats, at the front of the aircraft, and the best service, the aircraft was crowded, and uncomfortable. After much lobbying, and complaints from civilian staff, this system was modified later. The plane landed at Ankara and Bombay for refuelling, and comfort stops, before arriving at Singapore, and we were glad to disembark We were taken to the 'Chequers' guest house, where we were able to settle and acclimatise. Until my Ford Classic (registered SP1347) arrived, I obtained lifts into the Naval Base with colleagues, and Muriel, and Neil, used the cheap and plentiful taxis for shopping. A colleague, Maurice Hodge and his wife Joan, with their daughter Judith, arrived at the guest house just after us, and Muriel with her previous knowledge of Singapore, was able to show Joan around. They also became friends, with whom we shared holidays, and evening card schools, and we learned how to play Mah Jong, from them.

After a short time, we rented a bungalow in Lewis road, owned by an Indian Mr.Sabapathy. Our neighbours on one side were a Royal Marine officer, who worked at the Naval Base, his wife, and two small children. They also had a very nice mongrel dog, named Smokey, who came with the house. He was very discriminating, and was able to differentiate between black people, who he didn't like, and barked at, and white people, who he just wagged his tail at. On the other side, were an Indian family, while opposite, we had a small Malay Mosque. At lunch time every Friday, (their holy day) dozens of Malay men (no women), appeared in their traditional dress of Sarong, Kebaya, and Songkok, for their weekly prayers. We enjoyed the daily call by the Mezzuin, from the tower of the Mosque, which had been converted to modern technology, and was in the form of a recording. The bungalow at 11 Lewis Rd. was just off the Bukit Timah Rd., at $4^1/_2$ milestone, but as the main Naval Base was approx. 20 miles away, and was reached more directly via the Thompson road, we always used that, rather than the Bukit Timah, which ran directly to the Causeway to Johore, but required a long journey of about 4 miles, through the Naval Base

On the Thompson road there were numerous Kampongs, (collections of dwellings) where Chinese families lived in wooden huts, with attap roofs. The women washed their clothes at standpipes, situated at the edge of the road, and the children usually went barefoot. When the children went to school however, they were dressed in blue and white school uniforms, which were spotlessly clean. At one of these kampongs, we often saw an old man, taking his pig for a walk, on a lead. There were two reservoirs, the Pierce, and the McRitchie, set out as English type parks, which were very pleasant to sit in. The Thompson road passed through Nee Soon village, which contained a local army depot, and was well known for the many "ladies", who operated there. The other villages on the Thompson road were Canberra, and Sembawang, where there were gates leading directly into the Naval Base. Sembawang was just outside the Naval Base residential area, and had a row of local shops, where we did a lot of shopping for local goods, and souvenirs, and where Toothy Wong carried out his tailoring, and dressmaking business. I joined a car pool, to get to work, as this saved on petrol, and wear and tear on the car, and I managed to arrange separate transport for Neil, and a couple of friends, instead of the school bus, as Neil on occasions did not feel too well on the bus,

Our Cook/Amah at Lewis Road, was a Cantonese called Wan Tai, whose uniform was a white blouse, and black trousers. She was an excellent cook, and her curries were superb. Like most Chinese, she favoured boys, so Neil got rather more attention than Rosemary. A picture of Wan Tai and the children, in the garden of our bungalow, is shown at Fig.25. The bungalow was situated just off the Bukit Timah road, which had huge monsoon drains, along each side. During the monsoon season, the drains often overflowed, and on a number of occasions, the water came part way up our drive. When this happened, the noise from the bullfrogs was tremendous. A picture of the front of the bungalow and the Malay Mosque opposite is shown at Fig 26.

Once we had settled, we rejoined the Singapore Swimming Club, and spent most of our Sundays there, reverting to our old bad habits, of curry tiffin, and tiger beer, with the children resorting to cheese toast, smothered with tomato sauce. The cheese toast was the best we (and everyone else) had ever tasted, and although we never found out why, it was one of the most popular foods, for the children. Neil met one of his school friends Keith there, and Rosemary spent a lot of her time there with Andy, the son of one of our friends the Holloways. Neil and Keith seemed to spend much of their time, fighting in the water, while Andy and Rosemary, after they graduated from the children's pool, surprised and frightened everybody, by jumping off the Olympic diving board. Rosemary also had a girl friend, named Mary Lou. They looked so alike, that they were often taken for sisters. One Sunday when we had been in Lewis Road a short time, we returned to the bungalow, where Rosemary managed to lock herself in the lavatory. She was unable to turn the catch (which of course she had been told never to touch), so we had to call on the fire brigade, who arrived with a large fire engine, with bell ringing, and the firemen in full fire fighting gear, who proceeded to chop the door down with an axe. We got the door repaired quickly by one of the Naval Base contractors, and never told Mr.Sabapathy, who would have been horrified.

Our khebun (gardener) at Lewis road, was a Malay boy called Ahmed, one of whose jobs was to shin up the coconut tree in our garden, and release coconuts for us. He always seemed to get one or two more than we asked for, and guess who kept those? He was a real character, and tried to get time off for all the local festivals Malay, Chinese, Indian and Christian. We soon disabused him of that idea. We had a very attractive garden, with bougainvillea round the front windows, and apart from coconuts, we had sugar cane, and a banana tree. We held a lot of excellent parties at the bungalow, especially at Christmas, and these were returned by many of our friends. Muriel remembers Peter Elsey (my co-driver and friend) and I, visiting one of the 'Worlds' for a party, and coming home by taxi, and rolling up the drive, very much the worse for wear, but happy with it. It was at this bungalow, that Rosemary lost her very favourite teddy bear, when a child visiting next door, threw it into the monsoon drain. In spite of many washes it never recovered, and a new teddy had to be provided.

Muriel decided to have driving lessons, and take her test. Michael Lim was her driving instructor, and he used a Morris minor for the lessons. As with all driving tests in Singapore, she had to overcome the hazard of the monsoon drains, China Town, and the parking test outside the Police headquarters. On her first test, Muriel just touched a pole when parking, and so failed, and the whole test had to be taken again. Fortunately the second test was successful, and she was able to drive the 'Classic', which was to prove invaluable when we came home, for taking Rosemary to school.

In August 1962, we made our first visit to Fraser's Hill, for a holiday 'up country'. We joined our friends Arthur and Lillian Twigg, and Maurice and Joan Hodge, residing at the Admiralty Bungalow, The road up to Fraser's Hill, is a single lane, tortuous and twisting road, carved out of the hillside, so that on one side you have solid rock, and on the other, a drop into the valley, with no railings as protection. Visitors were required to go in convoy for safety, but a great deal of care was necessary. A number of old vehicles, mostly lorries, could be seen down in the valley, showing where unserviceable vehicles, had steered off the road. There was no room for passing on this road, so all vehicles had to wait at the top, or bottom, in a queue, until the last vehicle – an official baton holder- arrived, and gave the all clear. Fraser's Hill Station, had a cool English type climate, and there were plenty of English flowers, especially roses, surrounding the bungalow. At night we enjoyed a log fire. The views from Fraser's Hill, over the blue topped mountains and jungle trees, were magnificent, and the sunsets were spectacular, making for great photography. On the return journey we stopped at Segamat Rest house, for a break, and were able to take photos of the paddy fields. The numerous river ferries, all seemed about to sink, but in fact took a number of cars, and the Muar ferry, could take one bus perched precariously at an angle, so they must have been safe.

Although this was our second tour, we still enjoyed visits to the Botanic Gardens, where the monkeys were very active and cheeky. We also visited the Tiger Balm Gardens, which were very gruesome, but offered some unusual photography. The Kranji War Cemetery also warranted an occasional visit mostly for the photography. There was also a small zoo at Johore Bahru, but we considered this to be very sub standard, and once was enough.

When we moved into the Base, we once again chose to live in one of the modern flats, after a short interim period, in what were known as "Jacksons". These were very old wooden bungalows, and were only used as temporary accommodation, to facilitate the move into the Base. Wan Tai did not want to come into the Base, as this required her to be vetted and take a medical, and as she was over 60, she declined. We employed another Amah named Ah Eng, who was quite young with a reasonable command of English, lived quite close at Canberra village, and was happy to baby sit while we were out. She had every Sunday off, so if we went out on Saturday night, and returned late, I would take her home. In the Base, the ladies had a great social life, both as individuals, and in groups. As a group they visited the home of Admiral Luce, C in C Far East Station, at Lady Luce's invitation, and Muriel and I were also invited to lunch there, at Admiral Luce's invitation on another occasion. The regular RN bus service which ran daily to the centre of Singapore, for the personal use of families, was well patronise by Muriel and her friends.

Muriel again joined the Naval Base Church choir, and while she was a member of the choir, was confirmed by the Bishop of Singapore. The vicar was the Rev. McManaway, who was a very popular, and Christian person. When he returned to the UK after his tour of duty, his replacement was a womaniser, who spent most mornings on board ships, to get his free drinks in the ward-room. Neither he nor his wife and daughter, seemed appropriate as a vicar and family, and were not popular. I believe he was sent home early, as being unsuitable for the post.

At Xmas, the Naval Base contractors, as well as the trades-men, all wanted to give presents. Tay Koh Yat still ran the bus service to the Naval Base for the workers, so we were contractu-ally involved. but young Mr Tay, arrived at the flat, with bottles of drink for us, and presents for the children. We were not supposed to receive these gifts, but it was very difficult to refuse, and thus give offence, and usually, as long as you declared such gifts (after consuming the drinks of course) it was accepted.

In 1962, I was persuaded to join the Freemason's Lodge at Johore Bahru, where there was a mixed membership of Malays, Chinese, Indians, and Europeans, and this was to become my last associa-tion with Freemasonry. The Lodge was named Lodge Johore Royal, because the Sultan of Johore was a member, and the Lodge was accordingly, rather grand. In 1962, and later in1963, they held the usual Ladies night which Muriel attended. These were always a pleasure, because everything was done to make the evening memorable, and pleasurable for the ladies. Muriel certainly enjoyed them.

In August 1963, we again visited Fraser's Hill, this time staying at the Whittington Hotel. Our room mates were The Hodges again, and Roger and Janet Newton, and their daughter. On this occa-sion we broke the journey up country, by stopping overnight at an old house in Malacca. The owner was an old Englishman, who had lived in Malaya for many years, including the war years, so he had a wealth of stories to tell us, before we went to bed. While we were playing golf at the Fraser's Hill golf course, we were uncer-emoniously moved off the course, in order to let the Sultan and his party play through. Admittedly they were better players than us! Maurice rather fancied himself as a golfer, but I had no pretensions, preferring to play tennis, and all the family had a go at this. We had also planned a trip to Hong Kong that summer, on a RFA, but unfortunately there was a strike by the local MT drivers, and as I was in overall charge of transport in the Base, we had to cancel the trip.

About this time, I contracted what was known locally, as dhobi itch, caused by sweaty skin being rubbed by the starch in our white uniform shirts. As this is a form of impetigo, and is catching, I was rushed off to the BMH for treatment. Being in the officer's ward, each evening after dinner, we were given either a bottle of beer, or a measure of spirits—lovely. When Muriel went in later, to have polyps removed from her sinuses, she did not get the same treatment, and was somewhat miffed. Her treatment was very painful, when the dressings had to be removed, but as usual Muriel took it very well. She did however have some pleasure then, because it was just before Xmas, and she had some fun, designing and making, the Xmas decorations, for the ward.

   Quite often we would go into Singapore for parties, hosted by our contractors, where there was lots of Chinese food, and liberal quantities of drink, At these parties if someone called Yam Seng, you were expected to drink your drink straight down, and some care and subtlety was needed, to ensure you didn't get inebriated. Because of this, on these occasions, we would get one of the MT drivers from the pool, to drive us there, wait nearby, and pick us up at the end of the party, which meant we could enjoy ourselves, and not worry about driving home. I always employed a driver named Haroun, a Malay, who was always immaculately dressed in a Songkok and Sarong. We also had some hilarious parties at the Swimming Club. We usually had a table of 6 or 8, – the Harrisons, the Elseys, the Robbins, and the Holloways. The cry of "play up

Pompey" between our table, and that of another colleague, Len. Smith, was a regular feature of these dances. On one occasion at a particularly boisterous party at New Year, I drove away from the club, with Muriel in the passenger seat, with her feet out of the window. Fortunately it was very late, so we didn't meet any traffic police, and we arrived home at about seven in the morning, just as Neil and Rosemary were waking. We were in for a long day.

The best party which had ever been held in the Naval Base, was unquestionably the fancy dress party, organised by Peter and Liz Elsey, and ourselves. It was October, and everyone had to wear Halloween costume, such as ghosts, vampires, skeletons, cats etc. Every one entered into the spirit of the party games, and we had some very original acceptance cards. We ordered fish and chips in newspaper, instead of the usual party fare, and everybody had to eat this, seated on the floor. During the evening we took photos of every couple, and we got sets of the whole group, for anybody who wanted them. Everybody did, and all agreed that it was the best party they had ever been to. Four of the costumes are detailed in Fig 27.

Photography was a very popular pastime in Singapore, because of the many things you never saw at home. The firm Kodak encouraged this, and put on a very colourful and attractive presentation of Malay dancers, at a site in Singapore. These were not only original, but were performed in a setting appropriate to the actual dance. We visited on more than one occasion, and the place was always full. In the Naval Base, the Dockyard Players were formed, to present the Gilbert and Sullivan operettas, and they put on some very creditable performances. I always enjoyed singing, but wasn't keen on acting, so I never joined. Strangely one of the members had a terrible stutter, but once on the stage, he sang like a professional without any problem.

During our last months in Singapore, Ken, Greta's husband, was posted to Malaya, and he and Greta visited us at our flat in the Base, and stayed with us. Ken had to leave first, but Greta stayed for a few days longer, and sampled the sights of Singapore. We were members of the Red House, the Naval Base Sailing Club, where we were regulars, and where I occasionally officiated as Officer of the Day on sailing days. This required me to fire the starting gun, and I had a group of admiring boys, when I did this. On regatta days each year, when the Round the Island race was held, I was required to pilot the rescue boat. This was a fifty foot launch, and I enjoyed the experience, ably assisted by Neil, and any of his friends who could wangle their way aboard. One of the specialities of the Red House was the steak sandwich, and we all consumed many of these over the months. We held our farewell drinks party for our friends at the Red House, and my staff invited us to a farewell party at the Tai Thong restaurant in Singapore. The local staff loved these parties, and entered into the spirit of them, although there was a certain amount of sad talk due to our imminent farewell.

The tour eventually came to an end, and we were booked to fly home by RAF Comet. The garage had arranged for Haroun to drive us to Changi Airport, and he shed a few tears when we left. The flight this time was excellent, with plenty of space, and good service. We landed at Gan in the Indian Ocean, and at Aden for refuelling, before we landed at Brize Norton, where we stayed in RAF accommodation overnight. Next day we were taken to Reading station, and arrived at Elm Grove in Portsmouth, rather later than expected. My mum was concerned about us being late – we had a delay in Changi –and she came to Elm Grove to see what had happened to us. Elm Grove was again a temporary base, while we looked for another house in London. Yes I had been appointed to the Admiralty once again.

CHAPTER 13

Back to England

For personal reasons, we decided to stay at Elm Grove for only a short time, to avoid driving to London from Portsmouth, looking for a house, so after a couple of weeks, we booked a hotel in Surbiton, as a long term booking. It also made it easier for me to commute to work, as Surbiton was only 20 minutes by non-stop train, to Waterloo. The owner of the Arundel Hotel Mrs.Humphreys, had two children, a boy (Roy) about Neil's age, and a girl, slightly older than Rosemary, and they all got on very well together. The girl took Rosemary on her first ice skating trip, and the boys did what boys do!! One of my memories of this pleasant summer, was Fred. Trueman getting his 300th. Test wicket, the first player ever to do so. I think it was during this holiday period, that I took Neil to see his first Test Match at Lords Cricket Ground. .

I was appointed to the Admiralty building at Earls Court, so I found it easier to leave the train at Wimbledon, and take the District line underground to Brompton Rd., a few minutes walk to the office at the Empress State Building, a modern high rise triangular glass and concrete edifice. Our house agent Gascoine Pees, had an office in Surbiton, a short distance from the hotel, so we were able to check on new properties, daily as they came on their books, and we eventually viewed, and accepted, a property at 60 Pine gardens in Berrylands. The house was a thirties built, semi detached property, with a reasonable (60-70 feet) pleasant garden, with mature apple and pear trees. The road had wide grass verges, planted with numerous flowering cherry trees, which was particularly attractive in the spring. We were to stay in this house for 12 years, the longest we had been in one house since we were married. (Between 1951 and 1964 we had moved 5 times, and lived in 11 houses.)

Neil had done well at school in Singapore, and although Surrey education standards were high, he had no trouble in getting a place at Surbiton Grammar School. After a year or so in the old buildings, the school moved to a brand new building at Thames Ditton, a couple of stations down on the Hampton Court railway line. Now Neil and I both commuted from the local Berrylands station, me on the up line, and Neil on the down, so we could walk to the station together at 8 o'clock. After taking a while to settle in to the different routine at home in England, Neil enjoyed his school days at Surbiton Grammar, which did not change its name after moving to Thames Ditton Rosemary was only six when we arrived home, and she attended the local primary school, at Grand Avenue. Unfortunately her schooling had been of a very high standard at Singapore, and she found herself well ahead of the local children, which necessitated her having to mark time, a situation neither she, nor her teacher, found helpful, and this caused some bad feeling. This could have had some bearing on the fact, that when she was eleven, she was deemed to be only border-line for the grammar school, and she was allocated to Tolworth girls school, which didn't have a very good reputation. At the primary school, Rosemary learned a lot of little poems, which she recited to me when I said goodnight to her. I was then expected to recite these poems back to her, word for word, and when I failed, I was castigated in no uncertain terms. The poem I most remember is about a squirrel:-

Hey little squirrel are you ready for the winter?
Soon t'will be here then what will you do?
Summer's nearly past winter's coming fast
When the trees are bare who will provide for you?

The second verse escapes me, but I believe the squirrel does survive.

Muriel drove Rosemary to and from Tolworth school each day, although as she got older, she often walked home in the afternoon. Rosemary took up ballet lessons for a while, but this was soon overtaken by a new interest in horse riding. At Hampton Court Mews, the Horse Rangers of the Commonwealth had their stables, and Rosemary and her friend Carol joined together. They spent many happy Saturday afternoons riding in Bushey Park. Rosemary had a very good riding seat, and enjoyed galloping whenever she could. She also took part with a school friend, in numerous gymkhanas in the surrounding area.

Both the mums visited us regularly at Surbiton for holidays. This meant taking the car down to Portsmouth after work, staying overnight, and bringing them back in the morning. On one of these occasions, I remember starting off in the evening after snow had fallen. Road conditions were very treacherous, especially on the Kingston Bypass, and I was not looking forward to the ride over the Devil's Punchbowl, at Hindhead, on the A3. Fortunately there was not a lot of traffic about due to the snow, and quite suddenly as I approached Hindhead, the roads cleared and remained fairly clear, all the way to Portsmouth. Next day, I was pleased to see the snow near home, had virtually disappeared. On another occasion when I was bringing my mother up from Portsmouth, we encountered a runaway horse on the A3, but fortunately it ran past us, rather than at us. In 1960 Mum made one of her regular visits, and because Dad had been chair bound for some years, and needed help to move around, he went into hospital for care, while Mum was with us. Just after Mum got back to Portsmouth, Dad died in hospital, and was cremated at the Portchester Crematorium. In some ways it was a blessed relief for Mum, as she had lifted him around for a number of years, due to his worsening neuritis, which he had contracted, due to living in the trenches, during the first world war. Now Mum had 26 years relief, before she was destined to join him.

Muriel had passed her driving test in Singapore, but like me she had to retake the test, to drive in the UK. She was by now an experienced driver, and was expected to pass first time. Unfortunately on her first test, the driving school test car had a puncture, and the MOT tester, had to phone for a car, to rescue them both. Needless to say the tester was not amused, and she failed the test. The driving school immediately arranged another test, and this time she was successful, and she continued to drive, until she developed cataracts in both eyes. Because of these, she spent many hours at Surbiton Hospital, undergoing treatment, some of it very painful, and during this period she visited her mother who was in hospital in Portsmouth. I don't think her mum realised how difficult it was for her. .

CHAPTER 14

The later London years

While I was working in London, the Admiralty -now called the MOD(Navy)-decided to buy the Phantom aircraft from America. Because I was then managing naval American equipment, I attended the first symposium of the American Navy, and their contractors, in London. There were about 40 of them, and about 10 of the British contingent, because whereas we covered all aspects of equipment, procurement, for our Department, they were fragmented, and each delegate could only talk about the limited part of the project, for which he was responsible. As a result of this symposium, and the knowledge I acquired from it, I became one of the UK members, of the Integrated Maintenance Management Team (IMMT), responsible for the purchase, issue, and subsequent maintenance, of the electronic equipment, fitted in the aircraft, designated the Phantom F4K. When the project was up and running, a member of my office team was required to transfer to America, to join a UK procurement team there. I was the obvious choice, but unfortunately I had learned the American jargon so well, and become so knowledgeable, I had become too useful to my Director, who refused to let me go, and somebody else went instead.

While I was disappointed, what I didn't realise at the time, was that all the IMMT meetings, were to be held at various locations in America. Altogether I made 13 trips to the USA, including visits to Washington, Bayonne, and the Pentagon, with the US Navy, and to Philadelphia, Baltimore, and Boston, to the various contractors, employed on the project. We were always well treated at these meetings, and we were very popular with the ladies who said, they loved to hear our accent. On one visit to Boston, staying at the Holiday Inn Hotel, we asked for marmalade for breakfast, instead of the usual packets of thin jam. The receptionist had never heard of it, but promised to get some for our next visit, and when we arrived next time, sure enough, there it was. We were pleased to get it, and the girls in the hotel were delighted at our apparent pleasure. There were a number of items that our resident teams in the USA could not obtain locally, and we were always being asked to bring such item as marmalade, custard powder, gravy powder, Rowntree's jellies etc with us, as well as up to date newspapers. As a quid pro quo, the local procurement team did however have access to duty free stores, from the Washington Embassy, and I occasionally managed to get whisky and brandy at lower than airport prices, to go with my box of 50 King Edward cigars, which I invariably brought home, as part of my duty free allowances.

In September 1968 while I was working at Admiralty London, I applied, and was accepted by, the British Institute of Management, as an Associate Member. This was largely due to the management responsibility I was required to undertake for the Department, in respect of my membership of the IMMT, in the UK and USA. In January 1980 I was upgraded to full membership, and was entitled to use the letters MBIM after my name. I remember there were one or two more senior departmental members, who had applied unsuccessfully for membership, who were slightly miffed. After I retired in 1983 I no longer saw the need to continue my active membership which I allowed to lapse.

It was in Washington that I got stopped for jay walking (in a park). I had left the pavement to walk down the road into the park, where there was no footpath, just a grass verge. I was stopped by a police patrol car, and asked why I was walking (they expected everyone to be in a car). Although I explained that I was an English visitor, and had no car, this barely satisfied them, and it was suggested that I leave the park as soon as possible. I got the impression that they had never come across this situation before, but being English-enough said. Nevertheless I had to abort the walk, and go back to the pavement in town. On another visit to Washington, I had to spend the weekend there, and on the Saturday afternoon, I visited the White House. It was quite an experience, starting with meeting and talking to the Americans in the queue, to visiting the Oval Room, which we were allowed to look into, but not to enter- the guide carried a large revolver in a holster round his waist. I bought the inevitable souvenir book, while I was there. On the following Monday, I told my American colleague of my visit, and was surprised how few of them had been there. It is probably because Washington is largely a working centre, and staff tend to commute, as we do in London.

I also managed to visit the Pentagon Building, and was surprised to find that it was open to the public, and even had a few vagrants in the many corridors. The security of individual rooms leading off the corridors, was therefore inevitably tight, as one of my colleagues on the Polaris Programme, found out to his cost. He was found guilty of leaving his room unlocked, one night, and this was discovered by the security team. He was removed from the project, and sent home in disgrace, and because the incident was placed on his personnel record, he never got promoted again. Many of my colleagues at home envied, my numerous trips to America, but you can soon get disenchanted, with living out of suitcases, in hotels, and waiting in airport lounges. It was however a unique experience, and I am grateful that I had the opportunity.

When Neil left Surbiton Grammar, he was offered a Business Management course at Kingston Polytechnic. He decided he would like to leave home, and strike out on his own, so he moved in with his friends Jack, Nick, and Rob, to a flat owned by Jack's father. Neil still managed to come home at weekends, for his Sunday lunch, my beer, and to bring his dirty laundry for Muriel to wash. Although she didn't say much at the time, Rosemary really missed him when he left. The four lads were complete opposites, quite mad, and had a tremendous amount of fun together. The repartee between Jack and Neil, was particularly clever, as they both had a distorted sense of humour. Nick was very fastidious, and tended to be a mummy's boy, while Rob was famous for the enormous amount of baked beans he consumed, and the obvious consequences.

On one occasion the four of them decided to take a holiday in France, and Belgium, in a broken down old banger of a van. We were convinced it would never complete the journey, but apparently it lasted until they had just got off the ferry, on the way home. They decided to start the journey from our house. Nick arrived with loads of luggage, (including a dress suit), and was promptly told by the others, to take it all back home. It was probably just as well, as he had forgotten to bring his passport. They eventually got away much later than planned. They met some very nice people on their trip, and a girl wrote to Neil from Belgium, for some time after they came home. Neil's French was pretty good, so I expect he impressed her as the spokesman of the party.

While we lived at Pine gardens, we had a number of holidays. In 1967 and 1968, we had self catering holidays at Holimarine, a holiday village in Somerset. There was admittedly not a lot of amusement there, and on the second trip, Neil made his aversion to the holiday quite plain, so we spent a lot of time in the amusement arcades, to try to keep him happy. It was Neil's last family holiday with us, so when we went to Austria, Neil went on holiday with his friends. We stayed in the Hotel Pfaffenhofen, and spent a lot of time walking. Rosemary managed to find a riding stable close by, and enjoyed a ride on a rather large Haflinger horse, coming back just as the sun was setting. It wasn't till we got home from our holiday, that we learned Neil had suffered a bout of acute breathlessness, while on his holiday, and had to return home early. We believe that this was the start of Neil's breathing allergy, that he suffered from for many years

In 1973 we had a holiday in Alcudia, Majorca. The hotel Lago Monte, had a good swimming pool, which Rosemary used frequently, and there were a number of trips available around the island, which we took advantage of. This was Rosemary's last holiday with us. In 1975, Muriel and I went on holiday to Exford in Somerset, where we stayed in the White Hart hotel, Muriel's sight, due to the ripening of her cataracts, was by now poor, and she couldn't see very well, so our holiday was restricted to walking, and local visits to places, like Lynton, and Lynmouth. Although neither of the children came with us on this holiday, we were allowed to have Glen our golden retriever with us, in the bedroom. A local hunt pack exercised their hounds, passing the hotel in the early morning – we never heard them, neither did Glen. The food here was good and plentiful, as you would expect in the countryside, and our packed lunches, containing game pie, which we took on our walks, were excellent. This is where I became addicted to game pie. for life.

CHAPTER 15

The last of London

In 1968 I took up an appointment as a Staff Inspector, in The Civil Service Department, on temporary promotion to Senior Executive Officer. I was responsible for inspecting organisations, which employed Architects, Engineers, Quantity Surveyors and associated technical grades. This involved me in visits to Cardiff, Liverpool, Edinburgh and many other places in Britain. One of my trips required me, to inspect the work of Structural Engineers, from Scottish Departments, from Glasgow up to Inverness. Most of this work was involved with the structural safety of bridges, over streams and minor waterways, and remote buildings, and the inspection became a scenic route, of bridges, Lochs, and forests, in which the battlefield at Culloden, and Loch Lomond featured. I also joined a team of Army inspectors from time to time, and took part in inspections with them in Germany. On one of these, instead of flying, we decided to make the overnight sea trip, between Harwich and the Hook of Holland, and thence by train to Munchengladbach, for the first part of the Inspection. The second part was at Bielefeld, and we decided to take a flight in an army 2 seater reconnaissance plane. This was really sub standard tourist, with metal bucket seats, and because the plane flew at a low altitude, it turned into a very rough ride. I was glad to arrive at Bielefeld, feeling slightly sick.

Staff Inspection was a very interesting job, frequently on your own, and therefore quite responsible, but I was mostly away from home for the whole week, and only saw the family at weekends. As a result I was very busy at weekends in the garden. It was on one of these weekends, while I was mowing the lawn, that I chopped the end off my thumb, while attempting to remove an obstruction from the cutters. Unfortunately the engine 'skipped', and removed the end of my thumb. Neil found the missing end, and offered it to the nurses at the Surbiton hospital, where I was taken. They refused the thumb tip, because it was oily and dirty, so the next day the surgeon removed a small lump of flesh from my thigh, and grafted it on to the end of the thumb. It took beautifully, and although my thumb does not look quite normal, it has always been perfectly serviceable, and because there was a small piece of nail left after the accident, the nail grew again if slightly askew.

After 4 years of inspecting, I returned to the MOD(N), having got substantive promotion to Senior Executive Officer in 1969, in absentia. From 1972 I was manager of the Departmental Store Grades. When a rationalisation of these grades was undertaken, I headed up the team undertaking the review. The team visited all the R.N Dockyards and Depots, in the UK, and made two visits to Gibraltar. As I had not previously served in Gibraltar, this was a new experience for me. I seemed to spend rather a lot of time in various bars around the Island, especially at week ends. The Gibraltar tourist board operated regular ferry trips to Morocco, and I took advantage of one of these trips. Our party visited the Casbah, a collection of shops and bazaars, rather like Change alley in Singapore, where they seemed to offer almost everything you could think of. I became so interested in these shops, that I became separated from the main group. I was just wondering what it would be like to become part of the white slave trade, when I caught up with the group. Spain was making life difficult for the Gibraltarians in those days, especially at the frontier, but they remained strongly pro British, and I hope they will continue to be so. I also hosted the Stores Grades annual conferences in Edinburgh. During our time at Surbiton we continued to visit Norman and Doris, who had settled at Watford on their return to UK, and they visited us at Surbiton. Because we were working near to each other, Norman and I would make regular lunch time visits to Veeraswamy's, the best of the few curry houses in London at the time. Our visiting came to an end, when Norman was posted to Bath.

In 1976 Muriel's mother, who had been in St.Mary's hospital in Portsmouth, for a long period, died. She had suffered quite a lot, having had one leg removed, and in many ways, because her quality of life had deteriorated, her going was a blessing. Both Muriel and Greta had made regular visits to the hospital, but Greta lived in Andover, and Muriel in Surbiton, which limited visiting. Muriel especially, had cataracts in both eyes at the time, and travelling on the train was a huge problem. I don't think Gladys ever realised, how much it cost Muriel to make these journeys. . Muriel said afterwards how much she prayed to get through these times safely, and recalls that on a number of occasions, people thought she was drunk. There was however plenty of kindness shown by the sailors, who were going home on leave, and used the train. Better times were ahead however, after she had her first operation in Surbiton Hospital, earlier in the year and I can remember her delight when the hospital removed her bandages, and she said she could see the roses in the grounds.

On 31st.July 1976, Neil and Micheline got married. They had met, while they were both working at the John Lewis store, in London, during Neil's work related part, of his Business Studies degree.

The wedding was held at Christchurch, in Orpington, Kent. Jack Garwood, Neil's co-lodger was best man, and Rosemary was one of the four bridesmaids. Muriel bought a new hat, and was able to see everything that went on, after her eye operation, earlier in the year. Neil had invited Len and Yvonne Smith, and Ernie and Margaret Holloway, to the wedding, some of the old gang, that Neil had had so much contact with, in Singapore, and of course Neil's gang of reprobates from Surbiton, were very much in evidence. The reception was held at Micheline's parents home in Orpington, and we all thoroughly enjoyed the day.

CHAPTER 16

To the West Country

In September 1976, I had the opportunity to get away from London at last, when I was appointed to Bath. Neil was already living in Leeds, and working with British Gas, and Rosemary decided not to accompany us, but to stay in Surbiton, where she managed to get a flat, in the same house in Effingham road, where Neil and the boys had stayed. After some searching in and around Bath, we found a four bedroom detached house we liked, at 20 Littlemead, Box, which was within our budget. This house was more modern than our house in Pine Gardens, and had beautiful views from the front of the house. Sooty the cat, and Glen our Golden Retriever, travelled with us in the Ford 'Classic', which was now 15 years old, but still running well. We had a little difficulty selling the Pine Gardens house, as it was a 1930's semi-detached house, and I had had little time, to make improvements. We eventually found someone, who was happy with the condition of the house, and wanted to make the improvements himself.

When we moved in September, we stayed overnight, in Norman and Doris's house, at Lansdown in Bath, (they were away on holiday at the time), and moved into our new house the next morning. It had been a lovely summer that year, but from October, it rained steadily for months. Living now, only five miles from my office at Ensleigh Bath, I used the 'Classic', to drive there, and back. This was the first time that I had been able to do this, having previously always travelled by train to the office. There were plenty of fields and footpaths, on our doorstep now, where we could walk Glen, and Sooty caused some amusement in the road, when he would follow Muriel and Glen down the road, for their walk, and jump out on them from behind trees and bushes.

We soon found Littlemead residents, many of whom were about our age, to be very friendly and helpful, and for some years we held Xmas, New Year, and summer evening drinks parties, at each others houses. Norman and Doris now lived close again, and they came to dinner (usually a curry), and we visited them. Gradually as we all got older, these parties became fewer, but did not cease altogether, and we continue to go to tea with Norman and Doris, and they visit us, to this day. Around 1978, I invested temporarily, in a fairly new used blue Morris Marina, and offered the Classic to Neil and Micheline. Micheline collected the car, and used it for a long time between Leeds and Rotherham, where she was teaching. These 20 mile trips along the M1 eventually brought the car to its knees, but it had served the family well, for almost 20 years. The Marina was always intended to be temporary, and subsequently I purchased a Ford Escort in Venus Gold, also destined later, to become a family car.

In 1979 I was promoted to Principal (Chief Executive Officer), and posted to Copenacre, an RN Depot, between Bath and Chippenham, as Assistant Director. I was now even closer to my office, (about 2 miles in the other direction, and about 10 minutes drive away). I had never before enjoyed such luxury. My new post had three separate but related parts, involving NATO Codification of R.N. equipment and spares. Firstly, I was responsible for the Policy and Procedures, of NATO Codification, for the Royal Navy. Secondly, I was the Royal Navy member (at Captain RN level), of a committee, headed by an Air Commodore, concerned with Inter Service rationalisation, and computerisation.. Thirdly, I inherited the Secretaryship of a NATO Committee, consisting of members of the British, Dutch, German, Danish, Norwegian and Belgian Navies. This latter post started me off on my travels again.

My job at Copenacre was largely office orientated, which brought its problems. I was in charge of approximately 100 Executive, Clerical, Technical, and printing staff, plus messengers, cleaners etc.(See Fig.28) I had to endure one strike of technical staff, which caused a stoppage of some of the office work, but I had a good relationship with the Staff Side, and Union representatives, and the strike was short lived, and passed of peacefully, and without lasting acrimony. I had one printer who was very 'Bolshie', and who enjoyed being awkward and aggressive, but he was suddenly appointed as a local Magistrate, and after that, his attitude changed completely. The only job I really disliked, concerned a Technical Officer, who was really sub standard, and after 2 letters, and 2 interviews, my senior technical officer and I, decided, after a number of inadequate reports, that he would have to be dismissed. Unfortunately this generated a Tribunal, which I, as senior officer was required to attend. Most of the members of the Tribunal were clearly on the side of the technician, and the lady member made it very clear, that even after 3 years of problems, she didn't consider we had exhausted all possible avenues. Fortunately the technician involved, was not offensive, and realising his shortcomings, admitted he found it difficult to do his job, to the required standard. His dismissal from the service was finally agreed, nevertheless it was an unpleasant experience for all concerned, and I could see why some people might suffer lower standards from staff, rather than go through this unpleasant procedure. My staff were generally cooperative, helpful, and friendly however, and we worked well together. One mitigating feature of the routine work, was that we employed a number of contractors to do the technical processing work, and this meant that occasional trips to the firms works, to monitor their progress, was followed by a free lunch in convivial surroundings.

The Inter-Service group, of which I was a member, was mainly concerned with the introduction of a new computer, which was intended to rationalise and be compatible with, all the technical codification equipment being introduced into the Services. Our meetings were held at an RAF Headquarters office, in outer London, and dragged on for years. The new computer and its programs, seemed to generate more problems, than it solved, and even after the project was supposedly complete, there were regular complaints from the technical staff, using on-line equipment, and these had to be resolved on an emergency basis, as they occurred.

At this time I was asked to write articles on NATO Codification, in the Naval Electrical Review, and the Journal of Naval Engineering. I also gave a presentation on the application of Codification in the Royal Navy, to the Army, at Woolwich Garrison The chief guests were the Vice Chief of the Defence Staff, General Sir Patrick Howard-Dobson, with Major General J.T.Stanyer DGSC, and my own immediate boss, Air Commodore J.R.Lambert. Afterwards the Army invited us all to a special lunch, in the Garrison Officers Mess. I still have the menu for this meal, and the seating arrangements.

Perhaps the most interesting part of the job, was being the Secretary of the NATO Committee, which comprised all of the Northern Navies (Germany, Holland, Denmark, Belgium, and Norway), who were involved with NATO Codification. All the other members were uniformed members of their respective Navies, of Captain / Commander rank, but the meetings were held in English, being the common language, hence my Secretaryship. Meetings were held every six months at alternating venues. This meant visiting Wilhelmshaven, Bergen, Copenhagen, Brussels, and Amsterdam. Meetings were always well conducted, and the delegates were made especially welcome in the evenings, when the liquor flowed, each country wanting to demonstrate the quality, and diversity, of its national drinks. I made some good friends here, and have some very happy memories, but as every other meeting was held in the winter months, I also had a number of frustrating waits at airports, while aircraft were waiting to be defrosted, or runways cleared of snow. On one of these occasions I arrived back in Heathrow so late, that all trains had ceased running to Bath, and I had to find a London hotel to stay in overnight, and catch an early train back in the morning.

In May 1982, the Department of National Defence of Portugal, decided that they wanted to join other NATO countries, in becoming involved with Codification of their materiel, and held a symposium at Pamela, in Portugal, to announce their intentions. As part of the event, we were taken to Pamela Castle, situated on a hill outside the town, for a celebration dinner. I still have the Ementa (menu), but unfortunately it is in Portuguese, and I can't remember what we ate. I do remember however that the meal was especially good, and the wine flowed freely. I also discovered that Portuguese brandy was foul ,the only thing that spoiled an otherwise excellent evening. Although the hotel we stayed in was perfectly acceptable, it appeared to be in the middle of a desert of scrub land of sandy soil, with stunted bushes, and no greenery. I decided that I didn't like the Portuguese countryside. The Portuguese airline that we travelled on, also left something to be desired, but Gatwick to Portugal was fortunately only a short flight.

After we had moved to 20 Littlemead, Muriel was offered an appointment at the RUH in Bath, to remove the second cataract from her eye. The operation was very successful. It had been quite a long and often painful time for Muriel, but she had borne all the difficulties without complaint, and now with her spectacles with special lenses, she could see normally again Over the years we had visited Neil and Micheline in Leeds on many occasions, and this allowed us to see many surrounding areas in the Yorkshire Dales, and to make visits to York, to see the Shambles, the Minster etc. and also allowed us to see the Grandchildren, Alex and Faye, as they were growing up. I normally drove, as Muriel had stopped driving when her eyesight began to fail, and on one or two occasions, we used the train, but eventually, I found the 4 hour car journey too much for me, and we then relied on the family visiting us instead.

On 13th June 1981, Rosemary married Michael Bishop at All Saints Church, in West Ewell Surrey. They had worked together at a pharmaceutical firm in Ewell, and Rosemary had got very involved with helping Michael's mother, who was not well, and who died shortly before the wedding. Micheline and Michael's sister Jane were the bridesmaids. The buffet reception was held at the White House hotel in Epsom, which turned out to have exceptional service, and lovely grounds, which the guests took full advantage of. The best man and a number of guests, were Michael's friends, but I can't remember their names. After the reception, a number of us went back to the house, in Ewell, where Rosemary and Michael had taken up temporary residence.

During my various trips to America on MOD(N) business, I had been unable to take Muriel with me, partly due to the fact she could not have travelled or stayed with me, but also because it would have interrupted the children's education. So in October 1981, we decided to visit the west coast of America, where my trips had never taken me, and we flew from Heathrow to San Francisco. We stayed at the Canterbury Hotel, which had a coffee shop/restaurant next door, and as the food here was excellent and plentiful, we used it for many of our meals, only venturing elsewhere for some evening meals, and getting our lunches on the hoof. San Francisco was trouble free, so long as you stayed away from some designated places, and we were able to walk around most areas. The climate in San Francisco, (the locals hate you to call it Frisco) is very temperate, and there are a lot of morning mists. Coach trips provided us with the local amenities, including the Golden Gate Bridge, and the Bay Bridge. We visited Muir Woods where the Redwood trees grow. These are hundreds of years old, and are huge. We bought a small souvenir dish made from the redwood, and there were numerous other artefacts you could buy. We visited the Fairford hotel, where they have lifts on the outside of the building, and we tried out their rooftop restaurant, with a revolving bar at the top. All we could afford there was one drink!!

San Francisco residents are not very complimentary about their northern neighbours, in Los Angeles, and vice versa. Nevertheless after a week in San Francisco, we flew to Los Angeles for the second part of our holiday. Los Angeles is a fantastic place, and as Muriel said, it's like living in a TV programme, or a film. The hotel we were to stay at, was on Sunset Strip, but this area had become quite seedy, so we were transferred to the Ambassador Hotel, on Wiltshire Boulevard. This was a dirt road in 1921 when the hotel opened, and the hotel was responsible for making it the main artery of Los Angeles.. The hotel has hosted Academy Award presentations, Gala Hollywood functions, and contains the famous Coconut Grove. Political figures like FDR, Truman, Eisenhower, Kennedy, and Johnson have stayed in the hotel, so we were in good company.

Like San Francisco, there were a few no go areas, as two girls staying at the hotel, found out. They visited an out of town Rodeo, and on leaving, were walking along the street, looking for transport back to the hotel. They were stopped by a police car, and severely chastised for walking alone at night. They were taken straight to a taxi rank, and the driver was instructed to deliver them back to the hotel. There is however so much that you can see, and do, in Los Angeles, The Hollywood Bowl, Fisherman's Wharf, Universal studios etc, and we tried them all. We were disappointed in the Hershey Chocolate Factory, their chocolate is not nearly as good as Cadbury's. We visited Disneyland, and tried a number of the less energetic rides, and film scenarios, but one day isn't really long enough to take it all in. We also visited another similar, but less exotic theme park, at Knott's Berry Farm, where some of the rides, like Montezuma's Revenge, were for the very brave, or very foolhardy, and were left severely alone. While we were at the hotel, Carol, Neil and Michelne's friend, contacted us and invited us out. Carol and her mother Barney collected us, and took us to an authentic Mexican restaurant, where we were serenaded by violinists while we were eating. It was all we could do to stop laughing out loud, but it was a very good evening nevertheless. Perhaps the only thing that spoiled Los Angeles, was the officious and surly immigration staff, at the airport. Carol said they were renowned for it, but this was a very small price to pay, for what was otherwise a fabulous holiday.

In May 1985, we took a holiday in Amsterdam. It was not a great success. Our range of hotels to choose from was for some reason limited, and the hotel we chose offered only bed and breakfast.

We had expected to have a fairly wide choice of alternative restaurant facilities, but because we arrived on a Sunday, we were limited to a Burger type coffee bar. Muriel perhaps unwisely, put her handbag down on the floor alongside her seat, and when we got up to go, she realised it had been stolen. Neither of us saw a thing, it was very expertly done. This meant a trip to the police station, to report the theft, so that we could claim on our insurance. Fortunately there was very little in the bag, mostly keys and cosmetics, and nothing that could identify our home address, our Passports being locked up in the hotel safe. Nevertheless it was a very inauspicious start to the holiday. We did subsequently find a good restaurant, which produced the best pea and ham soup we have ever tasted. You could stand your spoon up in it.

We made a visit to the Anne Franck Museum, and saw the hiding place, and the Diary, and we also had an interesting trip, to the Delft pottery factory. It was a rather wet holiday, and when we returned home, I suffered a bout of lumbago, which I put down to the wet weather. To put the kybosh on the holiday, the day we were returning, there was an airport strike, so we had to stay another night at the hotel, and find our way to the airport early the next morning. We were fortunate in obtaining seats on a flight to Gatwick, and from there we had to return to Heathrow, by airport bus, to collect the car which was garaged there. Not our best holiday by a long chalk.

CHAPTER 17

In Retirement

In January 1983 I was due to retire, but as an immediate replacement could not be found, I stayed on until May. I had already decided that I needed to keep myself mentally alert after retirement, so in September 1982, I enrolled on a degree course, with the Open University. Two foundation courses at first level were needed, to ensure that you were of an appropriate standard to complete the course, and I decided to take both of them (on Arts and Technology) in my first year, thus reducing the course length from 6 years to 5. My tutorials were held at Chippenham College, and later at Bristol University, and the course work was supplemented by TV and radio programmes, which could be recorded and studied at leisure. The course booklets and literature, were also accompanied by pre recorded tapes. For these foundations, courses you were required to attend a summer school for one week, and I managed to organise both of my summer schools at Bath University, which reduced my travelling. The end of year exams were held at Bath Technical College, and in spite of taking two courses and working as well, I managed to pass both.

I thus only had to take four more courses, one per year, to achieve my degree. These were second level history courses, covering 17th. century England, the Enlightenment in European history, and the changing face of modern Britain. My third level course, (required for honours degrees), was comparative themes of British and American history. I have always been interested in American history, and as this gave me some fascinating insights into slavery, and the North / South war, this was right up my street. Having been successful in all of these courses, I was awarded my BA degree. The degree ceremony took place at Exeter University in July 1988, and my scroll was presented by the then Chancellor, Lord Asa Briggs. Muriel accompanied me to the ceremony, and watched from the balcony of the hall, and afterwards we strolled in the grounds. All the graduates had the usual Cap and Gown photos taken in the hall, (Fig.29), took their own photos in the grounds, and we enjoyed tea in the refectory. We stayed overnight in a hotel in Exeter, and returned to Surbiton the next day, after a really excellent ceremony, and a happy day out.

In 1986, after a short spell in the Alexandra Hospital in Portsmouth, when her health deteriorated rapidly, my mother died peacefully aged 95. She was cremated at Portchester Crematorium, and her ashes were scattered in the Rose Garden, where Dad's ashes had been scattered, when he died in 1960. Both of them have an inscription in the Book of Remembrance. Mum had been the focal point of our family for many years, and all her children, grandchildren, and in laws, visited her regularly at Doyle Court, at different times. 'Grandma' was a loving and caring person, and I never heard her be unkind to, or speak ill of people. Pat and I had visited her in hospital just before she died, and as Pat lived next door, we were able to put her affairs in order quite quickly.

In the summer of 1988, the night before we were going on holiday to Jersey, I contracted severe pains in my right chest, and was taken to the Royal United Hospital in Bath, where I was diagnosed as having Gallstones. After a few days of treatment and a scan, I was sent home to await an operation, for Gall Bladder removal. The date they gave me was December 1988, which coincided with Rosemary's and John's wedding, so I asked for another date. Fortunately this did not involve much delay, and in January 1989, the Gall Bladder was removed. It doe not seem to have made the slightest difference whatsoever, to leading a normal active life.

Rosemary and John became friendly, when they worked together in London. John had taken his BSc degree in Aeronautical Engineering, at Kingston Polytechnic, and they both worked at a firm in Richmond, which made prosthetics (artificial limbs), for the NHS. Rosemary was living at Idmiston Square, at Worcester Park, and John joined her there for a while. Michael her previous husband, had been the most impractical person I have ever come across. John was just the reverse, and could seemingly undertake any task. Rosemary and John decided to get married, and chose Xmas eve 1988.

Rosemary had set her heart on hiring a coach and horse, instead of a car, to take her to the church, and as I was giving her away, (for the second time), I travelled on the coach with her. It was a lovely mild December day, so Rosemary was able to show off her wedding dress, without having to cover it up, with the white fur coat, provided for her. The journey to Saint John the Baptist church at Old Malden, where the ceremony was held, was fairly short, but we attracted plenty of attention. John managed to get hold of a video camera, and John's brother made a video of the service, and filmed afterwards, in the church grounds. Carsten a friend of John, was best man, but Rosemary decided not to have bridesmaids. Alex and Faye were the attendants, and were dressed appropriately. When we arrived at the church in the coach, Alex was very jealous, and said to me "you are lucky

Granddad". When Rosemary and John left the church for the reception, they decided on a circuitous route, and again attracted much attention, with lots of well wishes, and Merry Xmas calls. The reception was held at The Old Swan at Thames Ditton, right on the water front. The reception went very well, I gave the usual "father of the bride speech" and afterwards Muriel and I, and John's parents Jean and Jack, came back to the house in Idmiston Square, where we were all staying for the night. It was a grand day out, and everyone thoroughly enjoyed it. Muriel and I were sorry to leave the next day

As we had missed our previously planned holiday to Jersey in 1988, due to my illness, we decided to try again in June 1990. We flew from Bristol, and stayed at a small hotel overlooking the sea front, and promenade, which provided us with many pleasant walks. We had not visited Jersey since our honeymoon in 1947, so we were anxious to see if it had changed much. The hotel we stayed at in 1947 "Swansons" was still there, but now under a different name. We only stayed a week, but managed to fit in visits to various places of interest, including the Shire Horse Farm, and the Butterfly Farm. We also managed to fit in a trip to Sark No vehicular traffic is allowed on the Island, only horses and carriages, so we queued up for a trip round part of the Island, in one of these. Sark still had a Seigneur, and we visited the Seigneur's house. Apart from its own particular scenic beauty, Jersey has an excellent zoo, run by Gerald Durrell the zoologist, which houses golden lion monkeys, gorillas, lemurs, macaws, and even wallabies. We took lots of photos there. The boat trip was also a welcome change for us, and we considered the holiday to have been a great success.

An unexpected death occurred in the family, in December 1991, when Michae,l my nephew (Pat's son), died suddenly after a short illness with Cancer, at the early age of 54. Michael was a very popular person, both at work, and locally, and there were about 100 mourners at his funeral service. Michael was also cremated at Portchester Crematorium.

In an earlier chapter, I mentioned that I belonged to the Admiralty Male Voice Choir. After I retired, I decided that I wanted to sing again, and I joined Box Singers, as a baritone. A couple of years later, Muriel also joined, as a contralto. The choir specialised in presenting carols and Christmas music, at the very popular Village Christmas, given in Box each year. We also gave other choral concerts, and offered our services to churches, in the area. We had a wide repertoire, and although we did not consider ourselves to be a professional choir, (we always said we sang for pleasure), at one time we had over 40 members, but with a regular turnover of pianists, and conductors. Because we were an ageing group, and for other reasons, the choir numbers declined, to only about 20 members, and we latterly tended, to restrict our involvement to the Christmas concerts.

Muriel had been the Secretary of the local branch of the Cancer Research Campaign (CRC), for over 20 years, and was awarded a silver brooch to commemorate the fact. Muriel still worked as the Meeting Secretary for the group (now designated Cancer Research UK since the CRC joined the Imperial Cancer Research Group), but restricted her involvement in fund raising events. Muriel has since been awarded a Certificate, and a badge, from CRC headquarters, commemorating her 27 years of dedicated service, to Cancer Research fund raising activities, locally.

4 - 10 - 13

Dear Yvonne,

Thank you for sending me
Gordon Kennison's book.

A very detailed biography of
his life and memoirs.

The piece about his time
with Box Parish Council was
of interest.

Ian Lovell

CHAPTER 18

Civic Responsibility and Celebration

I n 1987 I was co-opted on to the Parish Council in Box, for 4 years, and served on various committees, chairing the Footpaths/Highways committee for 2 years. This brought me into contact with the Cotswold Wardens for the area, and between us, we led, and took part in footpath walks at weekends. As there are over 90 footpaths in Box, our scope was virtually unlimited, and we were responsible for the maintenance, and improvement of many of them. When the local elections were held in 1991, I was re-elected, and voted to be the Vice Chairman, for two years, by the other councillors, and then subsequently as Chairman, for a further two years. I had been responsible back in the 1980s, for persuading the Parish Council, at one of their Annual Public Meetings, to adopt all night street lighting in the Ashley area, for safety and security reasons. There were a few people who felt it tended to urbanise, what is essentially a rural area, but fortunately I had the support of the local constabulary, and with almost full support at the meeting, the Parish Council made the recommendation to the County Council Highways Department, who accepted it, and it is still in operation today. As a member of the Council, I now had the opportunity to propose Ashley, as a Conservation Area, within North Wilts. We were already included in an Area of Outstanding Natural Beauty (AONB), that ran from the Cotswolds, through Bath, to this area, but I was anxious to make speculative building in the area, less easy to achieve. For this I had 100% local support, and my proposals were readily adopted, by the District Council.

One of my duties as Chairman/Vice Chairman, was to read the lesson, and lay the wreath, at the remembrance service at St Thomas a'Beckett, the Parish church, on November 11th. I also visited schools, to tell them about the Council's duties and responsibilities, to discuss painting competitions which we asked the schools to undertake, and then to judge the entries. I was also asked to present the prizes, at events like the Junior Badminton Club annual meetings, and generally was the Parish Council representative, at any events in the village, where this was required, or requested. The chain of office was not very spectacular, but it was necessary to show it off on these occasions. Since my time, it has been expensively upgraded.

In 1994, the Parish Councils of England, had been in existence for 100 years, and for the Centenary celebrations, the Parish Council decided to prepare a presentation, for local residents. This consisted of various set pieces, to demonstrate visually, the activities of the various committees viz Footpaths/Highways, Planning, Recreation Ground, and Burial. (the Cemetery in the village is run by the Parish Council) As Chairman, my tas, was to demonstrate the history of the council, during the last 100 years. I managed to obtain from the County archives, all manner of documents, diaries, minute books etc, even a list of the original members of the Council, and the minutes of their first meeting.

As a permanent feature of the Centenary, the Council decided to restore the railings around the fountain, in the centre of Box. The fountain had been erected at the time water was first piped down to the village, and school, from wells situated on higher ground, above Box. The railings surrounding the fountain had been removed, not as we suspected during the war, but in the 1950's, when they had deteriorated, and the money was not available at the time to reconstruct, and refurbish them. To replace the railings we needed money, and by publicising the event, we gradually got sponsorship and donations, which allowed us to go ahead. A Chippenham ironworks firm., prepared a number of alternative designs, and after we had selected the best, we arranged for a sketch to be prepared by a local artist, and we offered one of these prints (mounted) to anyone who donated £100, toward our costs. I have a copy on the wall, in my dining room. I officiated at the opening ceremony, and Muriel made a video of the proceedings. At the end of my four year stint, I decided I had done my civic duty, and did not put my name forward for the 1995 elections.

During my time in office in May 1993, I suffered a heart attack I had been humping a heavy petrol mower over the back garden fence, to cut long grass, along the strip of our neighbour's garden, adjacent to ours, and my heart didn't like it. I was taken to the Royal United Hospital in Bath, with a "minor myocardial infarction" After a week of treatment, I was discharged, with a medication called Beta Blockers. As these still gave me minor Angina pains, I was readmitted to hospital in November, when my medication was completely changed. Since then, I have suffered virtually no Angina pains for many years. One of the outcomes of my second visit to hospital, was the recommendation that I should take regular exercise, either walking or swimming. The former was easier to undertake, and since then I have walked for about an hour each morning, without any problems. I am probably fitter now at 80, than I was when I retired at 60. In January 1993 I reached the 'Big 70', and both of our families joined us at 20 Littlemead, to celebrate the occasion. Neil and family presented me with a cricket statuette, (70 not out against the world), and Rosemary and family a painting of a Shire Horse, my favourite in the equine world. I believe we all had a good time celebrating.

In 1997, Muriel and I had been married for 50 years, and Muriel decided she wanted to mark the occasion. We booked the Methuen Hotel in Corsham for dinner, and invited 50 guests, consisting of family and local friends. We had a 2 tier iced cake, made specially, and the hotel put on an excellent buffet for us. Because the Queen and Prince Philip celebrated their golden wedding in 1997, Buckingham Palace sent us a signed congratulatory message on parchment, under the Royal Crest. This was framed, and on display at the dinner. Neil gave the first speech, and I responded. Neil, Micheline Rosemary, and John were on the top table with us, together with Alex , Faye, Tom and Jack. Pat, Shirley, and her husband John travelled from Portsmouth, Greta and Ken from Andover. John's parents Jack and Jean came from Charlbury, and Coral, Muriel's old friend in Surbiton, came from Gillingham, where she is now living. Norman and Doris our old friends of nearly 50 years, got the time wrong, and arrived late from Bath, but we were pleased when they turned up. Pam Robins, another old Singapore friend came, and stayed the night with a friend in Bath. Because we couldn't put up everybody who travelled, at 20 Littlemead, Rosemary and her family stayed with us, and Neil's family, Pat's family, and Jean and Jack, booked rooms at the Methuen Hotel, and stayed overnight. Everyone else lived locally, and returned home late, but we hope happy. It was great to get all our family and friends together, and the occasion was, we felt, a great success.

In 1999 Reg. my brother died. We had never been close, communicating exclusively by Xmas card. He spent his early years in the Army, and I remember him coming home on leave, and sharing my bedroom, and spending most of his time at one of the local cinemas. During the war, Reg. was a Sgt. Major in the RAMC, was wounded at Dunkirk, and spent a time in the Army hospital at Catterick. After the war, he worked at Vauxhall Motors at Luton, but having fallen for Beatie, his married landlady, and with her husband's displeasure, he returned to Portsmouth, where he had a number of jobs, and where he met his first wife Maisie, who had four children of her own. He later moved to Dagenham, and worked for the Ford Motor Co for a number of years, in the paint shop. I managed to get him an interview for the Civil Service, in London, but he and Maisie decided the salary was too low. This would have improved after a time however, and the Civil Service job had prospects, which the Ford job did not.. After Maisie died, Reg. married a lady named Dee, who I really didn't know at all, and they lived in Essex until Reg. died. Reg. did have a son with Maisie, who died in his teens, but he always kept in touch with Maisie's children, who lived fairly close, and they made all the funeral arrangements.

CHAPTER 19

Civic responsibility and Nausea

While I was still on the Parish Council in 1995, I was approached to see if I would take on the post of Treasurer, at the Selwyn Hall in Box, the current holder having intimated his intention to retire, during the next 12 months. I accepted, never realising the tremendous amount of work and pressure this would entail. The job was mainly book-keeping, receiving monies from hirers of the Hall, and paying out the cheques to cover the general running costs and maintenance. For the first three years the job was reasonably time consuming, but it helped to keep my mind alert. However in 1998, the Selwyn Hall Management Committee decided, that as repair of the existing roof of the hall would soon be necessary, it would be better to undertake a rebuilding job, which would provide a new meeting room, and extra storage space under a new pitched roof. And then the really hard work started! We would obviously need to seek funds for this project, so as Treasurer, I was responsible for preparing an application to The Lotteries Board, asking for a large donation to our funds (approx. £120,000), based on the building and associated costs, estimated by our nominated Architect. This 30 page document took me weeks to prepare, and a few months after our submission, we were told our application was unsuccessful. However the wording of the refusal, led us to believe that our application had only marginally failed, and that we should try again, slanting our proposals toward encouraging greater use of the Hall, by local organisations. We obtained the written support of all our local users, and this documentation was incorporated into our second application, which took me months to prepare. For this submission we were still using the original estimates, prepared by our Architect, for our first application.

After a long wait of nearly 9 months, while our second application was considered, in April 2000 I was finally informed, that we were successful, and that a sum of £127,414 had been awarded. With the sum of £20,000 which had been collected/donated locally, we appeared to have enough to start building. Disaster struck almost immediately. First we discovered that the Architect had not included VAT in his costings, believing this was not due, as the Selwyn Hall was a registered charity. Due to this error by the Architect, we now had a shortfall on our available funding, and would need to resort to obtaining further sponsorship funding, from the County and District Councils, and the Landfill Tax, as the Lotteries Board would not allow any deviation from the original building plans, or offer any more money. We eventually managed to get most of the extra money together, but still had to resort to a loan of £15000 from ACRE (Action with Communities in Rural England)

Our next problem was with English Heritage. Because the Hall is built on the site of a Roman Villa, they refused to let us start digging footings and drains etc, until they had made exploratory digging at these positions, in spite of the fact that the site had been extensively dug, when the Hall was built in 1966. They of course found nothing new, but delayed the start of building for some months, and then charged over £1000 for the privilege of their attendance. Three tenders were called for in December 2000, but as all of these were considerably in excess of the Architect's estimate, a fourth estimate was sought from a local builder, who wished to be associated with the village project, and between this builder, and the Architect, they were able to pare down the costs to an acceptable level, while retaining all the spatial aspects of the original proposal.

Building work finally started early in 2001. Further trouble was looming however, as the partners of the building firm had a disagreement, and some of them, withdrew from the firm. We were then committed to transferring the contract, which our Solicitor arranged, but again at a cost, with solicitors fees. This transfer did not greatly delay the building work however, which went ahead rather too slowly for our liking, and a number of our regular hirers cancelled their bookings, due to the state of the foyer and forecourt. One woman actually likened it to a building site!!! Heavy rain also caused some problems, especially in the Library, where some electronic equipment was damaged, and we had to resort to special gangs, to clean the hall from floor to ceiling, due to the amount of dust being created. For the 12 months that the building work was in progress, my job was to ensure that the sponsors released enough money, in time to meet the Architect's and builder's invoices. All the lesser sponsors would only release their funds piecemeal, based on completed work, certified by the Architect. Fortunately the Lotteries Board offered 50% of their award up front, but for me the whole of the building time was a balancing act, to ensure that we finished the work with a credit balance, in the Selwyn Hall accounts.   Although I had recommend to the Committee that we should take up the full £15,000 loan from ACRE, I finished up with sufficient funds, to start paying back part of the loan early in 2002.

Early in (2002), we held a house warming, inviting residents of Box, to see the new facilities and soliciting donations for lots of smaller items, to refurbish the hall. We had always intended to hold an official opening ceremony, and had negotiated for a "Royal" Consequently in April, HRH the Duke of Kent, unveiled the plaque officially opening the Hall. The Selwyn Hall Management Committee, were all presented to the Duke. He arrived at the recreation ground in a helicopter, which caused much excitement, and as he departed, all the children from the village school greeted the Duke with waving flags, and cheering as his car drove off. After he had gone, all the invitees (Trustees and local dignitaries) were offered small eats, coffee and champagne. (Yours truly provided the bubbly, but I managed to keep a couple of bottles back, to celebrate my forthcoming 80th. birthday) The morning had passed very successfully, the one discordant note being, that in order to restrict the number of people the Duke had to meet, spouses of the Committee, and trustees, could not be invited. Muriel did however accompany me to Sainsbury's for shopping in the afternoon. What more could any wife ask for?

When the AGM of the Selwyn Hall arrived in June 2002, I tendered my resignation as Hon. Treasurer. I had served on the committee for 7 years, the last two of which, had been extremely pressurised, and stressful. I had spent many hours each week in my study, controlling the building finances, in addition to overseeing the normal running costs of the Hall. Muriel was most supportive during this hectic period, but it meant that a number of things that we could have done together, had been put off, and our trips out together became almost non existent. The time had come to call a halt, and I was very happy to hand over the reins.

CHAPTER 20

The Latter years

We were now able to do more things for ourselves, in the house and garden. I continued to write these notes, with the intention of finishing what I had started, two or three years earlier. John (Rosemary's husband), had given me an old computer, which I had used extensively, for my Selwyn Hall work. I was now able to remove all these files, and use the computer for these notes, and also to update all my personal/financial details, which had been left in hard copy for some years. Also I was able to do a lot more reading, which I had always enjoyed, and of course I continued to walk every morning, something I had not given up at any time for my Selwyn Hall work.

Unfortunately we were not as free as we had hoped. FRED our black cross collie dog, who had become quite a character locally, and was extremely well known, was now over $15^1/_2$ years old, and the years had begun to tell on him. From being a lively active dog, he was now partially blind and deaf, and had contracted arthritis in his back legs, which affected his walking. He had also suffered a slight stroke at some time, which caused him to walk crab fashion, and move to the right, and in circles. He was still lively enough to wag his tail on seeing you, and was still outgoing enough to enjoy meeting people, and wanting to talk with them.

We realised that the end was near, and at last, on February 14th 2003,.he died. We were both inconsolable for a while, and Muriel shed many tears over the next weeks. We had rescued Fred from the kennels in Bath however, and had given him, (hopefully) a full and happy life. Muriel had him individually cremated, and his ashes remain with us, in a smart wooden casket, with his name proudly displayed on it, in the dining room. This enables us to remember him all the time, and with his photos also on show, to remember him, as he was at his very best.

In 1999 I had developed an ailment called Polymyalgia Rheumatica, and Temporal Arteritus. The cause of this is a reduction of blood flow to the muscles, resulting in stiffness and pain. For me it affected the neck, arms and thighs, and produced small shooting pains in the temple. Fortunately there is a relatively simple solution - steroid tablets - starting with a high dose, and gradually reducing hopefully to nil. I went through a couple of these cycles, but by 2003, I had stabilised at a low level of 4 mg., and I hope to reduce this to nil, in due course. What with tablets for Angina (which fortunately I rarely suffer with now), Aspirin to ward off strokes, and tablets to reduce Cholesterol, I should be rattling. I have also been diagnosed as being Diabetic, so I need medication for that, and must maintain a low sugar diet. However all this medication, offers a reasonable life style, and quality of life, so I shouldn't complain. At 80, I can still walk quite fast for an hour or more a day, and I sleep well. I have good eyesight, so can do a lot of reading, something which I really enjoy, and good hearing, so I can listen to my classical music. I no longer crave foreign holidays, – I have done enough travelling in my time – and a quiet life is all I require. Muriel for her part has developed Atrial Fibrillation, an irregular heart beat, and Osteoporosis, so she is not as agile as she was once, and does suffer some pain. Like me she also has to survive on tablets, but we are still surviving, and we have each other.Hopefully we have a few more years to enjoy this quieter style of life

As I take my morning walks, now usually alone, I remember a song which I sing, as being very pertinent.

> *Glad that I live am I ,that the sky is blue,*
> *Glad for the country lane and the flowers too,*
> *After the sun the rain, After the rain the sun,*
> *This is the way of life till the work be done.*

Songs my mother taught me

Sing hey, sing ho, wax and china are folly,
Its best of all, when down you fall,
To be a wooden dolly.

I've got a black dolly called Topsy, who doesn't like sleeping alone,
'Cause she's afraid of the white bogey,
but I'm perfectly sure there is none,
But Topsy is only a dolly, and doesn't know better you see,
So I put her right under my pillow,
when I take her to bed with me.

You shan't come and play in my yard,
you shan't climb our apple tree,
You shan't come and play in my yard,
if you won't be good to me.

Said Molly I've made up my mind,
that when these fine pegs I have sold,
I'll buy poor Johnny some socks some socks,
To wear when he cries with the cold,
to wear when he cries with the cold.

Little bird I have heard, what a pretty song you sing,
Flying high in the sky on your tiny wing,
Gentle Jesus makes you fly, and he loves us you and I, little bird

Little brown brother, little brown seed, are you awake in the dark?
Here I lie cosily, close to my mother, hark to the song of the lark.
Little brown brother, little brown seed,
what kind of flower will you be?
I'll be a poppy, all bright like my mother, do be a poppy like me.
What! you're a sunflower, how I shall miss you,
when you've grown golden and high,
But I will send all the bees up to kiss you,
little brown brother goodbye.

Duck a duck a dilly, you little silly, what are you doing down there?
Duck a duck a dilly, with your head in a lily,
and your little feet up in the air.

Tardy scholar is your name, tardy scholar you're to blame,
We are making fun of you ha-ha, we're deserving of a prize ha-ha,
Tardy scholar is your name, tardy scholar you're to blame,
For you know how well we know you, tardy scholar is your name.

Dickie bird dickie bird, pretty dickie birdie,
Would you like some crumbs to eat, pretty dickie bird.

(Mum sang these words to the tune of Heykens Serenade,
while putting out bread for the birds in the garden,
and watching them through the window)

Some of these words and sentiments may surprise you,
but you have to remember that they are about 100 years old,
when teaching and social conditions were quite different.

Postscript

2004 was a reasonably normal year, but 2005 turned out to be traumatic.

Early in the year Muriel was diagnosed with Cancer of the Colon, and was admitted to the Royal United Hospital, in Bath, in May. The operation was successful, but while recuperating, Muriel experienced further pain, and an

X Ray disclosed a perforation of the bowel. This required another immediate operation, which fortunately was also successful. After two major operations in one week, recovery was bound to be slow, but after transfer to Chippenham Community Hospital, for final recuperation, Muriel came home, after having spent five weeks in hospital. The operations took their toll, both physically and mentally, but thankfully, recovery was continuous, and Muriel is now well on the way back, to being her old self.

Also I had a minor stroke in August, and was rushed into the RUH, where fortunately, recovery was almost immediate, and various X Rays, and a brain scan, indicate there have been no permanent effects. Possible further attacks, are being controlled by medication, rather than the need for surgery. Murphy's law came into effect however, because the stroke happened on the day before Muriel's 80th. Birthday, and she had to go into the local Bybrook Nursing Home, while I recovered The staff there were extremely kind, and made her very welcome, and they produced a special Birthday cake for her. Also some of her friends and neighbours were very caring, and arranged to visit her, to celebrate her Birthday.

2005 has been our "Annus Horribilis", let us hope 2006 will be kinder to us.

We are Survivors

(Those born before 1940)

We were born before television, before penicillin, polio shots, frozen foods, Xerox, contact lenses, videos and the pill. We were before radar, credit cards, split atoms, laser beams, and ball point pens, before dishwashers, tumble driers, electric blankets, air conditioners, drip dry clothes, and before man walked on the moon.

We got married first and then lived together, (how quaint can you be). We thought fast food was what you ate in Lent, a Big Mac was an oversize raincoat and crumpet we had for tea. We existed before house husbands, computer dating, and Sheltered Accommodation was where you waited for the bus.

We were before Day Care Centres, group homes, and disposable nappies. We never heard of FM radio, tape decks, artificial hearts, word processors, or young men wearing earrings. For us time sharing meant togetherness, a chip was a piece of wood or fried potato, hardware meant nuts and bolts, and software wasn't a word.

Before 1940, 'Made in Japan' meant junk, the term making out referred to how you did in your exams, stud was something that fastened a collar to a shirt, and going all the way, meant staying on a double -decker bus to the terminal. In our day cigarette smoking was fashionable, grass was mown, coke was kept in the coal-house, a joint was a piece of meat you ate on Sunday, and pot was something you cooked in. Rock music was a fond mother's lull-aby. Eldorado was an ice cream, a gay person, was the life and soul of the party, while aids just meant beauty treatment, or help for someone in trouble.

We who were born before 1940, must be a hardy bunch, when you think of the way in which the world has changed, and the adjust-ments we have had to make. No wonder there is a generation gap today ......BUT

By the grace of God we have survived.

꽃

With acknowledgements to Mr. Bridge.

The Hayden Family Tree

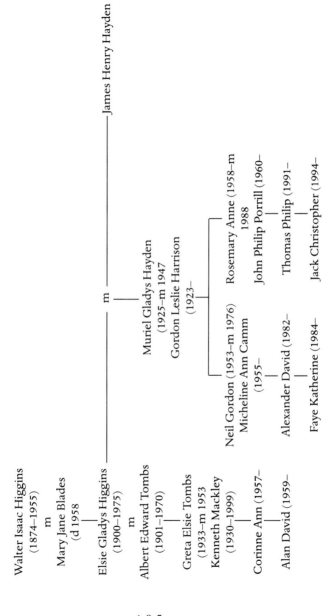

James Henry Hayden

m

Muriel Gladys Hayden
(1925–m 1947
Gordon Leslie Harrison
(1923–

Neil Gordon (1953–m 1976)
Micheline Ann Camm
(1955–

Alexander David (1982–

Faye Katherine (1984–

Rosemary Anne (1958–m
1988
John Philip Porrill (1960–

Thomas Philip (1991–

Jack Christopher (1994–

Walter Isaac Higgins
(1874–1955)
m
Mary Jane Blades
(d 1958

Elsie Gladys Higgins
(1900–1975)
m
Albert Edward Tombs
(1901–1970)

Greta Elsie Tombs
(1933–m 1953
Kenneth Mackley
(1930–1999)

Corinne Ann (1957–

Alan David (1959–

The Harrison Family Tree

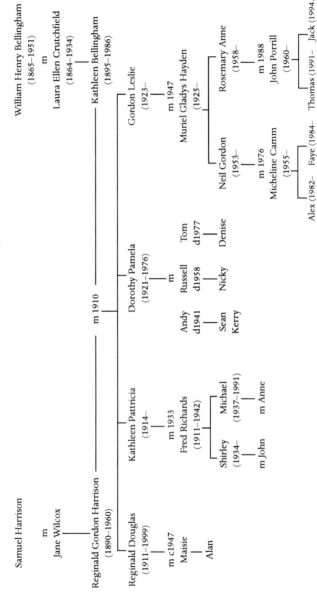

Lightning Source UK Ltd.
Milton Keynes UK
UKOW050327020713

213091UK00001B/54/A

9 781905 529889